"*Muslims, Christians, and Jesus* ▮ ▮▮ biblically trustworthy. I canno ▮▮ theologically praiseworthy study."

—Dr. Vernon C. Grounds, Chancellor, Denver Seminary

"So much of our training about sharing Jesus with others has an artificial, even adversarial tone. This book strikes a different and refreshing note. You might not agree (at first) with everything Carl says but you can't afford to ignore his message."

—Steve Moore, President & CEO, The Mission Exchange & Keep Growing, Inc.

"I've known Carl Medearis for many years and have constantly been challenged by the quality of his life and ministry. His heart for those who don't know Jesus is evident to all."

—Mike Bickle, International House of Prayer of Kansas City, and author of *Passion for Jesus*

"I have experienced Carl's compassion for people first-hand. His wisdom and experience give him unique insight into... sharing Christ with the Muslim world."

—Ted Dekker, bestselling author of *Skin, House,* and *Three*

"Carl Medearis is one of the most authentic Christians I know. I have spent time with Carl in the Middle East, and my own view of Muslims has been shaped by Carl's living example. I was very moved when I was released from prison, to find that Carl wanted and tried to come to Iran to negotiate my release. I would highly recommend his books so that others can be changed like I have been."

—Dan Baumann, author of *Imprisoned in Iran*

"Medearis takes an admirable task here: to teach us the gospel's, not the government's, perspective on Muslims. There is a lot to reflect on as he shares his perspective in this thoughtful work."

—*Advance*

"[Carl Medearis] writes with humor, authority, and wisdom on the power of Jesus to draw people to himself, from whatever background. His new book will leave you empowered and inspired."

—Daniel Morris, consultant and author of *The Pattern of His Presence*

"With a gracious spirit, *Muslims, Christians, and Jesus* attempts to outline the differences in these monolithic faiths, and help churches see the most important issue at hand is not assigning blame to terrorist organizations but rather, how do we love people to a real relationship with Jesus. You won't be able to put it down."

—Andy Braner, President of Kanakuk Colorado, author of *Love This!* and *Duplicate This!*

"My longtime friend Carl Medearis has helped me understand so much concerning the world of the Middle East. His message is not theoretical but is borne out of a life lived passionately for Jesus in a 'for all to see' lifestyle."

—Randy Sutter, Sr. Pastor of Vineyard Christian Fellowship, Cottonwood, Arizona

"This is a book deserving to be read and pondered and acted on, even if the only Muslim contact is a colleague at work."

—*The Lamplighter*

Muslims,
Christians,
and Jesus

Muslims, Christians, and Jesus

Gaining Understanding and Building Relationships

Carl Medearis

BETHANYHOUSE
Minneapolis, Minnesota

Cover design by Dan Pitts
Cover photo by Nicole Gibson, *www.nicolegibsonphotography.com*

Published by Bethany House Publishers
11400 Hampshire Avenue South
Bloomington, Minnesota 55438

Bethany House Publishers is a
division of Baker Publishing Group,
Grand Rapids, Michigan.

Printed in the United States of America

In keeping with biblical principles of creation stewardship, Baker Publishing Group advocates the responsible use of our natural resources. As a member of the Green Press Initiative, our company uses recycled paper when possible. The text paper of this book is comprised of 30% post-consumer waste.

green press INITIATIVE

Library of Congress Cataloging-in-Publication Data

Medearis, Carl
    Muslims, Christians, and Jesus : gaining understanding and building relation-ships / by Carl Medearis.
        p. cm.
    Summary: "A guide to gaining understanding and building connections between the world's two largest religions, written from the perspective of a Christian who has lived and worked in Islamic countries"—Provided by publisher.
       ISBN 978-0-7642-0567-5 (pbk. : alk. paper) 1. Christianity and other religions—Islam. 2. Islam—Relations—Christianity. 3. Islam—Doctrines. I. Title.
    BP172.M394   2008
    261.2'7—dc22

                                      2008028254

To Chris.
This book is as much your story as it is mine.

Without you I wouldn't understand people
or love God like I do.

ACKNOWLEDGMENTS

Two friends have encouraged me for years to write down these thoughts for others to read: Ted Dekker and Floyd McClung. Thank you, dear friends, for believing in me and for pushing me to stop running long enough to sit quietly and write.

Also a huge and special thank-you to my dear friend Samir K. You helped me understand Jesus in new ways and introduced me to the Arab world at a level far beyond my capability. You're the best.

TO THE READER

Meet Carl Medearis, my friend. In May 2003, just days after Saddam Hussein's statue was toppled in Iraq, Carl called me from Basra to tell me an amazing story of what happened after a sheikh asked him, "What are you doing here?" You'll find that story, "The Basra Sheikh," in this book. You'll also get to read one of my all-time favorite stories, "Being a Hope Broker." Listen when Carl says, "What I find most effective and most Christlike is to stay focused on Jesus."

To have such great stories you know there has to be a catch, and *this is it*: Jesus is the person behind Carl's experiences. Jesus is the catch. Jesus is creating a new humanity, a new citizenship, made up of all who have faith in him, whether they call themselves Christians or Muslims.

Jesus is the draw. Not Carl, not you or me. More of Jesus, all of Jesus—the Jesus of the Bible. In the history of the world who but Jesus could say, "Don't be afraid; you believe in God, believe also in me. I go to prepare a place for you, that where I am you may be also." Of whom else did men ever say, "Even the winds and waves obey him." Who but Jesus spoke with his dying breath, "Father, forgive them, they don't know what they have done." Only Jesus ever said, "Your sins are forgiven," thus disturbing the religious leaders but setting sinners free.

Jesus Christ is not "great" in the way we describe Alexander the Great. He is Jesus Christ the Only. And to draw people to Jesus you need . . . well, you need Jesus. The real Jesus is discovered in people's homes, where real friendships grow. Carl's book takes place in living rooms. It's a dialogue of love and respect. And right now the people of Jesus are much in need of loving and respecting Muslims.

I hope you've sat in a living room with Muslim friends. My Muslim friends are Kurds. I had the privilege of living in Kurdistan, Iraq, during the 1990s. They taught me a lot about love and respect. Then in 1997, when hundreds of Kurds came to the U.S. as refugees, I started a nonprofit organization, Friends of the Kurds, to help them resettle in Seattle. Dozens of American families opened their homes and hearts to the new arrivals—tired, poor, and yearning to be free.

The next stories about Muslims, Christians, and Jesus will be written by you and other readers. Don't hold back when the Lord tells you what to do and say.

BOB BLINCOE
U.S. DIRECTOR, FRONTIERS

CONTENTS

FOREWORD

Some people feel they need an enemy. We like to know who the bad guys are. Many Americans grew up watching simplistic Westerns. Everyone knows the bad guys wore black hats. For a long time, Communists were the guys in black hats, especially the Russians. Since the Russians are no longer the threat they once were, a new enemy was needed.

Muslim terrorists came on the scene just in time to provide some of us with a new set of bad guys to fear and hate and fight against. There are genuine bad guys: the Bin Laden variety. The trouble with having a common enemy of bad guys to fear and hate is that we tend to stereotype all Muslims and put them in the same category. When we stereotype, we don't see people—just images of people. The truth is that Muslims are moms and dads and soccer players and entrepreneurs and young ladies in wedding gowns.

In other words, they are normal people, like the rest of us. People God loves.

Have you noticed that through the life of Jesus, sometimes our enemy is changed and becomes one of "us" and God changes our hearts in the process? Through the love of Jesus, the Sauls killing Christians become Christians loving other people killing Christians.

Obviously, there are really bad guys. And our governments should do all they can to protect us. The problem with the war on terrorism is that it can put us on the defensive. God is looking for people who will go on a grace offensive, people who forgive and reach out in love. If we don't respond in faith and love, we miss what God is doing, and we miss our part in it.

In an effort to help us understand and reach out to ordinary Muslim people, Carl Medearis wrote *Muslims, Christians, and Jesus*. I love this book because it does not promote fear and hate. It does not stereotype Muslims.

Muslims, Christians, and Jesus is the best book I have read about Muslims and Islam. As you read this very human book, you will gain insight and compassion and faith. You will learn how to share your faith as a follower of Jesus in ways that show respect and at the same time are effective.

In a sense, this is a book about Jesus. Jesus loves Muslims. And you will too when you read *Muslims, Christians, and Jesus* with an open heart and a seeking mind.

FLOYD McCLUNG
INTERNATIONAL DIRECTOR OF ALL NATIONS

INTRODUCTION

This book began in 1983, when I first went to the Middle East. Back then, the majority of Americans, like me, knew little about the Middle East or Islam. The Reagan administration was in its first term, and Communism and the Cold War crowded the headlines. Baath-party socialist Saddam Hussein had been in power for only four years, and the secular government of Iraq was at war with its Shi'ite neighbor, the Islamic Republic of Iran. The news also brought us occasional stories about the Afghan campaign against Soviet troops, Libya's Muammar Khaddafi as a top-shelf bad guy, and the Ayatollah Khomeini, who had replaced the CIA-sponsored Shah of Iran. Still, there was little to no fear or suspicion of Islam in the West, mainly because the reality of terrorism was not yet on our doorstep. All was quiet on the Middle-Eastern front.

Until 2001.

As the world watched smoke and ash spew into the Manhattan sky on September 11, 2001, I was (ironically) busy teaching a bunch of students in Kansas City about loving Muslims. In fact, I had just drawn a diagram on the white board showing how we so often think in an *us-versus-them* paradigm. I was literally erasing the line between the words *us* and *them* when someone burst into the room in tears telling us what had happened. The next week, our family returned home to Beirut on one of the first flights out of a deserted Chicago O'Hare airport. For days after our arrival we received a steady stream of visits and calls from friends saying how sorry they were. One friend, Ahmed (not his real name), came by our house, slumped into our couch, and rubbed his face with his hands. "Carl," he said, "these terrorists have seriously hurt the peace we have worked so hard for."

"What do you mean?"

"America will go to war," he said, shaking his head, "and I am afraid that it will not end for years."

"I know."

"The West does not understand us. They see an Arab and they feel fear. They hear talk of Islam and they are suspicious. I am afraid that things will spiral out of control and that hatred will grow between my people and your people." He sighed. "Again."

"Ahmed," I said, looking him in the eyes, "we are each other's people. We are both followers of Jesus, friends of God, and brothers in a way that boundaries cannot take from us." A tear slid down his face and he tried to wipe it away before I noticed.

My family and I lived in Lebanon from 1992 until 2004. If 9/11 was going to rip the world apart, we were going to do everything we could to stop it. We had worked long to build friendships, and the last thing we wanted was to let them be torn away by international politics, hatred, and misunderstanding.

In 2003, I made two trips into Iraq. The war in Iraq had torn up the status quo by the roots, and my Iraqi friends were practically pleading with us to come over.

It was surreal, to say the least. At the border, we halted at a coalition checkpoint and for the first time in years I heard the Midwestern accent of an American in the middle of the desert: "Welcome to Iraq; may I take your order?" The troops were enthusiastic—GIs doing their job. We shook hands, exchanged pleasantries, and hit the road again, southbound for Basra.

A few weeks later, my life nearly ended, along with the rest of the team. As we returned north on the route at 160 clicks per hour, we were overtaken by a black Mercedes with one notable distinction: rifles. We were forced to the shoulder and escorted out of sight into the sand, below the lip of a *wadi*—a dry riverbed. There we were dragged from our vehicle, then lined up in the sand on our knees, hearts pounding and palms sweating.

Let me tell you, when an AK-47 stares at you, you find

an incredible capacity for introspection, along with a unique closeness to God.

I asked myself, *If I had to do it all over again, would I spend my life in the Middle East, living among Arabs, trying to be a visible expression of Jesus to them?*

I had my answer immediately. The Holy Spirit spoke inside of me so strongly that my body trembled. I heard the words *I love these people.*

That's when I realized the truth: I loved these Arabs too. But it wasn't *my* love that drove me—it was his love for them. I was simply a part of the story.

When my wife and I returned to the United States, we found that everyone wanted our opinions on the meaning of world events. It seemed that almost no one knew what to do, what to say, or even what to hope for.

I began to realize that because so many people were left wounded and vulnerable from the 9/11 attacks, they found it relatively easy to assume terrorism was synonymous with Islam, making it justifiable in their eyes to beat our plowshares back into swords. I know this is an observation that does not include all Westerners, Americans, or Christians. I also know I am treading on sensitive ground with this subject. But the causes of men were falsely aligned with the causes of God, linking our military successes to his will and broadcasting the message that God is "on our side."

At least that's how my Arab friends saw it. *The Christians are coming. Again.*

After we had moved back to the United States, I received invitation after invitation to speak at universities, churches, and other places. I was puzzled by my newfound popularity. One day I realized the truth. It wasn't *me* that people were interested in; a thirst had awakened, a desire to become more familiar with this religion called Islam. My ego wasn't deflated at all. In fact, my heart surged with hope. Many Christians are now choosing the road less traveled, driven to learn about Islam and thirsty to see if there is a way to reach out to Muslims.

In fact, when I'm asked—as I often am—what is the answer to the issues in the Middle East and I answer "Jesus," I am often mocked as being simplistic, even by my committed Christian friends.

They are looking for a political answer that simply doesn't exist.

When I can't make sense of something, I pull everything back to its simplest point, stripping away the confusion and noisy complexities. What matters is what has always mattered:

Jesus.

Maybe you're reading this book because you want to understand your Muslim friend or neighbor. Maybe you want to go to the Middle East to share Jesus' love with people. Maybe you're just curious about what makes a Muslim different from you. In any case, my intention is to give you some information to help you befriend a Muslim and practical tips on how to live a life that's truly Good News to a Muslim. I cannot hope to speak for every perspective on every issue. I'm not infallible, I'm not the final word on Islam. I'm only a follower of Jesus who loves Muslims. This book is not intended—in any way—to be the complete and final treatise on this matter; just helpful and genuine.

I've had Muslim scholars read each of these chapters, and they have agreed that what I've said is fair. At the end of many chapters are sections entitled "A Christlike Perspective," which are what I believe would be a response sanctioned by Jesus Christ. For those of us looking to live our lives as much like Jesus as possible, I lay out what he might want us to do with the subject at hand.

Throughout the book you will also find sections called "A Story of Faith," where I recount some of our family's most special experiences. Many occurred during our times in the Middle East, but I believe they will provide important insights—and inspiration—for the interactions and friendships you might have with Muslims anywhere.

CHAPTER 1

Before the Pillars: The Foundations of Islam

In the late sixth century A.D., a boy was born in Mecca, Arabia. His father was already deceased, and his mother would die when he was six. From these circumstances the boy would grow into a man who would unite the Arab people, wage military campaigns, and become revered as a prophet to millions of people for over a millennium.

His name was Muhammad. He is one of the most well-known individuals in all of human history, and his name is synonymous with the modern personality of Islam.

Outside of Islam and its reach, Muhammad is held at arm's length in the interest of scrutiny and theology. Recent observations have shed much light on his person, his language, his culture, and his shaping. The latter is of primary importance to scholars, evangelists, and apologists who wish to either explain his ways or reject them. Regardless of this scholastic influx, it must be said that first and foremost, Muhammad was a leader of men. Today, the religion that bears his mark is arguably the world's fastest-growing religion, with 1.4 billion adherents. Muhammad was obviously a visionary teacher.

Not much is known of Muhammad before his fortieth year, but historical studies of the period can fill some gaps. His birth city, Mecca, was an important hub for trade routes and enterprise. It was a through route for caravans and also held an important position in the maritime trades, providing a product and financial clearinghouse of sorts for both India and Africa. It is speculated that Muhammad was involved with commerce from an early age, taking business trips to as far as Syria before he was fifteen.

Although Muslims regard the era of Muhammad's birth and childhood as the end of a time of ignorance, there was, without doubt, a platform of various religious beliefs and practices in Arabia. The Arabs of the period were largely pantheistic, and many were idolatrous, worshiping a variety of deities and idols. Christians as well as Jews had also settled in many places in Arabia for purposes of business and expansion.

Nevertheless, the shrine of Mecca—the *Kaaba*—already was a recognized religious center for Arabs. The Kaaba is a haven for a series of sacred stones, the most important of which is the Black Stone, believed to have come from heaven. The Black Stone is built into the eastern corner of the Kaaba, and annual pilgrimages require the sojourners to come before it and perform various rituals. At the time, though, as many as three hundred deities may have been worshiped at the Kaaba.

Early Jewish and Christian cultures had an impact on the Arabs, which is evident in the Muslim holy book, the Qur'an. The Jews shared their beliefs with their Arab neighbors, as did the Christians, spreading at least a superficial understanding of the religion of the one God and the man Jesus. Many stories in the Old and New Testaments are also found, at least in part, in the Qur'an, including the creation, the fall of Adam and Eve, the flood, the birth of Jesus, and Jesus' performing miracles.

THE LIFE OF MUHAMMAD

Although nothing was recorded about Muhammad until over a century after his death, Muslim scholars report that he was raised by his grandfather and uncle, in the tribe of his family, the Quraysh, who were, at the time, responsible for the care of the Kaaba. Thus, the influence of religion began during his earliest years.

According to legend, Muhammad was in a caravan when he met a Nestorian monk. The Nestorians call themselves "The Church of the East." They are the only people on earth who still speak the Aramaic language of Jesus. This monk believed that Muhammad was a prophet, and supposedly told him so.

Later on, Muhammad married a prominent woman, Khadijah, who was fifteen years his elder. Because she was wealthy and well connected to the trades, Muhammad became a man of importance by managing her caravan. He was a member of the guild at Mecca, as well as a prolific traveler. He traded stories and discussions about God and religion with many Jews and Christians, fervently absorbing as much information as he could. Muhammad and Khadijah had seven children together, six of whom died young, with no surviving sons. After Khadijah passed on, some twenty years later, Muhammad would marry a dozen or more women.

It is important to consider that Muhammad was, at least in the beginning, a man with a desire to discover God. As he circuited Arabia, discussing God with the Christians and the Jews and the pantheistic and idolatrous Arabs, he grew disillusioned with the likenesses of God that were available to him.

By the age of forty, Muhammad was becoming more and more concerned with the sacrilegious practices around him. He felt that mankind was straying from the path of God, that people were diluting the truth and falling away from true religion.

According to tradition, Muhammad found a cave on Mt. Hirah, not far from Mecca, and he used the solitude of the place to meditate. It was during these meditations that he heard the voice of God, or, as some believe, the messenger of God, Gabriel the archangel (who is referred to as "the Holy Spirit" by Muslims).

Muhammad was given a series of messages that he believed were from God; he also believed that he was meant to give them to others. These messages were compiled some time after his death and formed into the Qur'an.

Muhammad kept his ideas and activities secret for a time, but as soon as he went public, the majority of Mecca wanted nothing to do with him. His message was extreme, and he promised that God would judge those who did not listen and obey. Those who did follow Muhammad's teaching were called *Muslim*, which means, literally, "submitted to God." Because he was vocal about the primacy of the one God, he was considered a threat to the Kaaba and the businesses around it, many of which thrived on the city's religious culture.

In the beginning, Muhammad and his followers were persecuted. The people of Mecca were violent, and their aggression was condoned by the leadership of the city. Before long, Muhammad and his family of believers moved to Yathrib (later renamed Medina), which was across the Red Sea from the Christian kingdom of Abyssinia (roughly modern-day Sudan and Ethiopia). There the people were more open to hearing the teachings of this new prophet. At first, both Christians and Jews were quite receptive to Muhammad, mainly because he was adamant about the sovereignty of the one true God and insisted that worshiping other gods would bring judgment and wrath.

It is at this point in history where *Islam*, meaning "to surrender" or "to submit," transitioned from a family-sized cell into the beginnings of an actual religious movement and was institutionalized. The Muslim calendar began in A.D. 622. Subsequent military successes brought so much plundered wealth to Muhammad that more and more tribes joined themselves to him. Muhammad wrote in the Qur'an a chapter—The Anfal, which means "the plunder of war"— to describe this phenomenon. There were some seventy-six of these battles during Muhammad's lifetime.

The presence of Christianity and Judaism was at first of no consequence to Muhammad. In fact, Muhammad is known to have preached and supported the veracity of the claims of the Torah, the words of the Jewish prophets, and the teachings of Jesus. But over time, it became clear that Muhammad was a different sort of prophet altogether, so the Jews failed to hold him in the esteem he desired, and because the Christians already had prophets, apostles, and a messiah, Muhammad didn't fit. After some time Muhammad found himself speaking primarily to his own tribal countrymen.

By the time of his death in 632, Muhammad had unified the Arab people, provided them with religious teaching and codified law, and given them military victories. By the 730s, Islam had spread as far as Spain and France, and whole areas had become Muslim, including Syria, Iraq, Egypt, Persia (Iran), Afghanistan, and all of North Africa (now Libya, Algeria, and Morocco).

Family Time With the Bedouins

One of the many things our Arab Muslim friends taught us is the power of family. Young Muslims usually live with their parents until they're married. The idea of being on your own at eighteen is unheard of in most of the Eastern world. And when young people do get married, it's normal to add a level to the parents' house so they can have plenty of space—right on top of each other!

Businesses are run as a family. At important meetings and gatherings, even weddings and funerals, small children often run among the adults. Muslims fight, love, are born, and die as families. Don't get me wrong, it isn't all roses, but it is different from the West. One of our most cherished values—individualism—isn't a known quantity to most Muslims. They would say, "If it's been good enough for our forefathers, it's good enough for us!"

This was a good lesson for our family in so many ways. We learned to serve together in a way we would not have likely experienced living in the United States. In Lebanon, our three kids were part of the gatherings in our home. They helped serve the dinners, and they even planned and organized events we hosted at community centers or in our home.

One such time was around Thanksgiving. We decided to give some of our toys to the Bedouin children who lived in tents in the Beka'a Valley (near Syria). We explained that the children were very poor and probably had no toys, while we had lots of toys. To our surprise (maybe shock is a better word), the kids came back with most of their best (read: most expensive) toys to give away. After my wife, Chris, and I recovered a share of our former godliness, we smiled and said, "Great, let's go."

We made the two-hour drive on the day after Thanksgiving. As we pulled up to one of the poorest camps we knew about, a mob of kids appeared seemingly from nowhere. They acted as if they hadn't seen a foreigner before. Running noses, bare feet, and big smiles marked these wonder-filled kids.

As soon as we told them we had gifts, about fifty more kids were suddenly hugging the trunk of our car. Honestly, we felt a bit overwhelmed. Funny how "serving the poor" often isn't the feel-good experience we expect!

I have no idea why, but we thought of singing them a song in Arabic before we gave out the presents. I think the fact that they were kids emboldened us—since we're not exactly the Von Trapp family. We tried to think of a children's song that we all knew and could sing in Arabic, which limited our choices to about . . . one.

"I have the joy, joy, joy, joy down in my heart. Where? Down in my heart." Know it? Well, that's what we sang. What a sight it must have been.

But the funniest thing was this: The word for joy sounds like "farrah." But the word in Arabic for mouse is almost exactly the same. The difference is so subtle that we didn't know we were actually singing, "I have a mouse, mouse, mouse, mouse down in my heart."

We couldn't figure out why the kids thought the song was so funny, which of course, led us to sing it louder (which is what one does when you're not being understood in another language). I can imagine the fires that night in the camp. "Mustafa, did you hear those silly white people singing about having a mouse in their heart? And they thought it was so cute. What was the point of that, I wonder?"

Anyway, we figured it out about a year later.

After we sang about the mouse in our hearts, we gave out the presents and then told them that God loved them.

I doubt any one of the children had an amazing experience with God from that encounter, but it was sure good for our family. And maybe that's not so bad.

WHO IS ALLAH?

It seems that Muhammad never intended to start a new religion. He did not consider Islam to be his creation. Rather, he considered Islam to be a call to return to the one true God, the God of Abraham—to submit to *Allah*.

It is vitally important to know that *Allah* is Arabic for

"God." Many people wrongly believe Allah is the name of *a* god whom Muslims worship—that Allah is a pagan god or some other strange deity. In fact, the word *Allah* was used by Arab Christians during Muhammad's time, and it is still used today. Christians in the Arab world—even as you read this—pray to Allah every day. They're praying to God. When any true believer prays in Arabic, God *is* Allah, and Allah *is* God. Moreover, every translation of the Bible into Arabic uses the word *Allah* for *God.*

There are some who disagree and contend that the word *Allah* comes from a pre-Islamic name for a moon-god. The word may have connotations from earlier usage, but even if this is so, those meanings have long since lost their definitive quality. *Allah* comes from the Arabic root *Al-Ilah*, which simply means "the god" or "the deity."

The word *Allah* is linguistically related to the Hebrew word *Elohim* and is also related to the Aramaic *Elo* and *Alaah.* The Aramaic word Jesus used on the cross when he cried out to the Father was *Alahi* (or *Eli* in some English translations), which was linguistically closer to the Arabic word for God than our modern use of the English word *God*, which derives its roots from the pagan Germanic word *Gut*, and, before that, from the Farsi (Persian) word for God still used in Iran and Kurdistan today, *Khoda.* Our English word *God* came from the Middle East!

In my reckoning, there is nothing helpful in telling a Muslim he or she believes in "the wrong God." What may be true, and definitely more helpful, is to show our Muslim friends how they can believe in God more fully in and through Jesus Christ.

People at the Edge of the Sea

The house was gone—swept into the Mediterranean Sea. It was one of thirty houses destroyed the night before in a horrendous storm that hit the Beirut coast. As we sat in the living room of one of the "good houses," drinking coffee for a couple hours, I found myself once again feeling helpless and asking God *why?* These were nomadic Bedouin Arabs who had been displaced during the Lebanese civil war and had built a shanty town along the seafront just five miles from where we lived. And now, even their makeshift huts were gone.

For me, the day had started off relatively uneventful. I had been trying to give each member of the Lebanese parliament and cabinet a New Testament and then pray with them. Some of the times had been so encouraging, others just hard work. On this particular day, I arrived at a member's house alone—all the friends I had lined up to come with me had dropped out one by one. It was pouring rain, I was hungry, and I didn't want to be there. Going up the stairs I muttered a relatively tired prayer, "God, help!"

I entered a smoke-filled office teeming with men, each wanting something from the minister. I fumbled around and mentioned that I was just bringing a gift— that I didn't need anything from the minister. After ten minutes he came over to me and politely said, "How can I help you?" I told him that I'd come to simply encourage him, pray for him, and give him a gift. When he saw the Bible, his eyes lit up. "This is the best gift I've ever received."

Nearly every time we've given the Bible as a gift, the appreciation has been overwhelming. Gift-giving in general is highly valued in Muslim cultures, and the Word of God is greatly respected.

We looked through the New Testament together, we talked a bit about how God surely wants to rescue Lebanon from her woes, and I asked him how I could pray for him. He asked if I'd heard about the three hundred people who had lost their homes the prior night. I said no. He had just met one of them and was sending some food, but they were going to freeze that evening unless they got blankets. I asked if I could help. . . .

The next thing I knew, I was scrambling for a couple thousand dollars, and later that very day we bought a truckload of blankets and delivered them. The people were beyond grateful. In this little spot on the beach that I never knew existed, only five miles from our house, we now have friends for life.

Late that night, the minister called me at home. "Thank you," he said. "What you've done is what Jesus would do. Whatever I can do for you, just let me know."

It's funny how right smack in the midst of our weaknesses and insecurities, God works. We just have to say a simple yes.

A CHRISTLIKE PERSPECTIVE

The most important thing we can do as followers of Jesus is to do just that. Follow him. Jesus himself is the Good News. The message that we carry is Jesus. Not church, not capitalism, not democracy, not doctrine, not the religion of Christianity, not Calvin, not Luther, not Democrat, not Republican.

If we truly wish to be able to build a relationship with a Muslim friend, the most important thing we can do is to follow Jesus' lead. Jesus had compassion for people, and he valued the same quality in his disciples, even above personal sacrifice.

If we begin with the attitude that we are going to debunk "all of that Islamic stuff," we'll be done before we get a chance to introduce Jesus, because we will have turned away somebody in the process.

Some suggestions when beginning a conversation:

Don't insult Muhammad, and don't be flippant with religious phrases or with God or your Bible. *Show respect, and you may well be respected for it.*

Do everything you can to keep it from becoming a me-versus-you debate. *Or a my-religion-can-beat-up-your-religion diatribe. That's not how Jesus spoke to others, and we would do well to follow his example.*

Show interest in your Muslim friend's faith not as a means of deception, but because you are interested

in them and what they think about God. *In fact, keeping the conversation on common ground and about everyday spirituality will prove to be far more effective than confrontation. Many Muslims are uneducated regarding their religion, and any attempt to force a theological point will end in shared frustration.*

One thing you will notice about Muslims in the Middle East, in particular, is that the Eastern perspective on logic is totally different from ours in the West. For example, when I first arrived in Beirut, I attempted to use C. S. Lewis's tried-and-true "Lord, Liar, or Lunatic" approach with my new friends. I said that because Jesus himself claimed to be the way, the truth, and the life, he was either who he said he was, or he was lying about it, or even worse, he was delusional. Those were the only options. It was either true or not.

"No," my friends said, shaking their heads. "He was a prophet of God, and he never told lies and he certainly wasn't crazy."

"Don't you see," I would plead, "the only option left is that he is Lord."

"No. He was something else. You need more options in your argument."

"There aren't any," I said, palms sweaty. "I'm being logical, and Jesus was logical."

That raised some eyebrows.

Only later did I realize that they had raised an interesting point: Jesus had lived in their region, spoke a similar language, and had similar ethnic qualities. And then Carl the Great White Missionary flew across the world to tell them that Jesus was logical. . . . That's just like an American.

Be genuine and patient. *Whatever denomination or church we come from, it is not our job to "secure converts." In bolder terms, we are not even here to "build the kingdom" but rather to obey the king. Kings build their own kingdoms, and Jesus surely can build his. We are involved in the process because we follow him.*

When speaking with a Muslim about Jesus: Use his title as a term of respect, i.e., "Jesus the Christ" (or Messiah). *This is actually a term that Muslims accept, and it shows a sense of reverence.*

Many Muslims are pleasantly surprised when they see someone praying, reading a Bible, or treating religious things with a sense of devotion. *In the West, we are so used to the separation of church and state that in public we acclimate to the nonreligious norms within our culture. Muslims see this as a blatant disregard of devotion to God. Many of my Muslim friends are surprised when I tell them that the president or some public figure believes in God. They don't see it in the media, where talk of God is rare, and devotion toward him seems nonexistent. Within Islamic nationstates, the opposite is true. Every Islamic state (even* *the secular ones) is permeated with religious devotion and/or tradition. Every public figure is a Muslim. Except for those in Lebanon, every political office carries with it some influence of Islamic law, to one degree or another.*

We don't want to wear our devotion on our sleeve, but we are free to be people who are obviously seeking to follow the ways of God and be more like Jesus. This is how we desire to live and what will pave the way for many genuine friendships.

CHAPTER 2

The Teachings of Islam: The Articles and Pillars of Faith

Muslims are obliged to acknowledge certain articles of faith, known as *iman*: objects of doctrine. According to Islam, there are several absolutes that every good Muslim must confess with his tongue and believe in his heart. Commonly this is said, "There is no god but God, and Muhammad is his prophet." A more complete form goes like this: "I believe in God, his angels, his books, his prophets, in the last day, and in God's predestined will."

On the whole there's really nothing disagreeable about

this statement. In fact, it's similar to a church's statement of faith.

The Bible places a high value on many of the same articles. Where is the difference? In a side-by-side comparison, the Muslim statement of faith is missing one primary thing: Jesus.

The most important thing we have to offer to our Muslim friends is Jesus. He's who we need. He's who they need.

Having said that, Muslims already *believe* in Jesus. He is considered the holiest prophet of Islam, born of a virgin, and now alive in heaven, waiting to return for the day of judgment. But I'm getting ahead of myself. Let's get further into iman.

THE SIX ARTICLES OF FAITH

1. First, there is God. There is one true God, and there is none other. The Muslim believes that the *oneness* of God is of primary importance. He is unique, he is whole within himself, lacking nothing. He has no equal, he has no division.

Many Muslims believe that the Christian idea of the Trinity "lessens" God, and that it is an offense against God to believe he is divided in any way. This can partially be attributed to a misunderstanding. Muslims often believe the Christian Trinity is composed of God the Father, Jesus, and the Virgin Mary. Muslims, however, do not elevate any person to the stature of God—not Jesus, not Mary, not Muhammad. In fact, it is offensive to say anything about

God that could be construed as irreverent or that indicates he shares his authority with anyone. Muslims believe that if you make a person equal with God, you have committed an unforgivable sin, known as *shirk,* or blasphemy against God. This one true God is all-powerful and all-knowing, with complete authority, and he is ready to judge.

Christians, when they first encounter the differences between the Muslim and Christian perceptions of God, are often tempted to begin introducing the "Christian God." I believe this is an unnecessary step—even a mistake. Why?

God is who he is.

Of course there are misconceptions and even lies *about* God, but none of them change the reality of who he actually is. By attacking the Muslim understanding of God, we may endanger or delay the possibility that the fullness of God, to be found in Christ, can be revealed to our Muslim friends by the Holy Spirit. This is how Simon Peter knew Jesus was "the Christ, the Son of the living God. Jesus replied, 'Blessed are you . . . for this was not revealed to you by man, but by my Father in heaven'" (Matthew 16:16–17).

Pressing our theological differences, especially at the outset, won't gain us a hearing. A recent study (whose authors prefer to remain unnamed) showed that the overwhelming majority of Muslims who came to faith in Jesus Christ and began following him did so because of personal spiritual revelation and through miracles. Very few embraced Jesus due to the use of apologetics or through doctrinal debate.

Once again, we see that faith in Jesus comes by seeing

him, being touched by him, being led by his Spirit, and not through intellectual argument.

A deep and thorough understanding of the Scriptures is vital for us to effectively point our friends to a complete understanding of who Jesus is and why he came. But always be careful not to let the understanding of doctrine take the place of a living relationship with Jesus Christ.

2. The Angels. Angels are the servants of God. Through these servants, God reveals his will, most notably to the prophets. According to the Qur'an, the greatest of the angels is the archangel Gabriel, the one who revealed God to Muhammad and who strengthened Jesus.

A different kind of angel-like being is the *jinn*. To quote the Qur'an: "And the jinn race, we had created before, from the fire of scorching wind" (Q 15:27).

The jinn are notable in that they are not men, they are not angels, and they can be either good or evil because they are believed to have free will. Accordingly, jinn can be either saved or condemned. There are many who fear the jinn. They are often connected with disasters and accidents and are believed to haunt abandoned places and deserts. Some Muslims will do whatever they can to avoid the jinn, which leads them to act out a variety of superstitious protections. For instance, some will hang a horseshoe above their door to keep the evil spirits out. Or they hang a baby shoe from the back of their car to keep the evil eye (through the jinn) from attacking their children. Many Muslims, particulary those who practice so-called folk Islam, have their tea or coffee cups "read" after they're through drinking, or take part in palm and tarot card readings and other things we would consider white magic.

According to Dr. Rick Love, folk Islam, not orthodox Islam, is generally the more popular form. Love writes in his book *Muslims, Magic, and the Kingdom of God,* "Folk Islam takes a more spiritualistic orientation to life. Spirits and demons, blessings and curses, healing and sorcery are its domain. . . . Its concerns are primarily heartfelt, not cognitive, and focused on the here and now. The issues of well-being, success, and health consume its time."[1]

Muslims also believe in the devil. In Arabic his name is *Iblis* or *Shaytan.* Traditionally, he is labeled as a fallen angel or a jinn, and to Muslims he is as evil as he is to Christians.

3. The Holy Books. This is one subject I cannot emphasize enough: Muslims treat their holy books with *great* reverence. Contrast this to many Christians, who, for example, commonly set their Bible on the floor beneath their chairs or keep a Bible in the bathroom. A Muslim would never do this with the Qur'an. They do not underline verses or write in the margins. Their books are holy; they are representative of God, because they are his truths. The actual words in Arabic are holy in themselves.

---

[1] Rick Love, *Muslims, Magic, and the Kingdom of God* (Pasadena, CA: William Carey Library, 2000), 21–22.

When you are sharing the gospel with a Muslim friend, be sure to respect both the Bible and the Qur'an. Use a clean Bible, treat it with extra care and respect, and do not put it on the floor or write in it.

Islam's holy books are:

The *Taureh,* which is what we would call the Torah, or the Pentateuch.

The *Zabur,* or the Psalms of David. David is considered a prophet, and his poems are considered holy.

The *Injil,* or the Gospels. These are the teachings of Jesus of Nazareth, which the Muslims revere as holy.

The *Hadith.* This is not simply a single book that is considered holy by all Muslims. Hadith are a series of traditions and precedents set in place by Muhammad's life. These traditions are many and varied, and there are varying levels of reverence for them. Some of these sayings and actions of the prophet are recorded (there are six "official" collections of Hadith), and all are called Hadith. Some are so serious that they are considered a valid basis for state law—even for legislation and enforcement. Others may seem trite, or even silly, to non-Muslims. Make every attempt to approach the Hadith with an open and respectful mind: A misguided laugh or joke could set back your friendship.

The *Qur'an.* This is the holiest book in Islam. It is considered the final and complete revelation of God to men. According to one particular verse in the Qur'an, called the verse of abrogation (Q 13:39), all later verses supercede earlier ones. To Muslims, this also includes teachings prior to the Qur'an. Thus, in Islam, because the Bible was written before the Qur'an, it is subject to the Qur'an. So in a case of disagreement—i.e., the Bible vs. the Qur'an—the Qur'an "wins."

Muslims will often say that Christians and Jews have distorted their original texts from God, and that is why the Qur'an is both necessary and "more correct." However, the Qur'an itself does not say this. (The next chapter highlights key scripture references.)

4. The Prophets. The Muslim understanding of the prophets is that they are the men God used to influence history and to be mouthpieces for his teaching. The prophets served as guides to keep men on the path of righteous living. The prophets have a prominent role in warning humans of the imminence of judgment as well as the consequences of earning the wrath of God.

According to Islam, of all the prophets, six are considered major prophets: Adam, Noah, Abraham, Moses, Jesus, and Muhammad. Because Muhammad is the last and final prophet, he is regarded as the "seal of the prophets," the one who has rendered all prophecy complete and final.

Jesus (*Isa* in the Qur'an) is regarded as the holiest prophet, without sin, born of a virgin, and, interestingly, called "his word" (Q 4:171). In Q 3:55 it even states that those who follow Jesus are superior to those who reject faith. None of the prophets, while they are considered role models for mankind, are divine.

What's astounding about the adherence to these prophets is that Muslims are not permitted to deny any of them. Read the list of these prophets again and note that all but Muhammad are in your Bible.

5. The Day of Judgment. This is the greatly feared day in which God will weigh every man's deeds and determine his eternal fate. In the Qur'an, the day of judgment is linked to the resurrection, and there will be warnings, very similar to the revelations to John on the Isle of Patmos. There will be natural disasters and wars and even an appearance of the antichrist. Following this, the resurrected ones will walk the earth for forty years, while the recordings of their deeds will be weighed. (This is orthodox belief but not common in folk Islam.)

Every person will then cross a narrow bridge. Good Muslims will be saved instantly, and some Muslims will fall into hell for a short period of time. All infidels (people who don't believe in God, which according to the Qur'an does *not* include Christians or Jews) will fall into hell and stay there for eternity.

6. Predestination. Because God is supreme and all-powerful, fate is understood to be predetermined by God, and therefore his will is final and absolute. Because of the predominance of this article of faith, the philosophy of fatalism has become widespread and pervasive among Muslims, who frequently mention *muqaddar,* or, as we would say in English, "It's been decided." For a Muslim, the concept of

THE TEACHINGS OF ISLAM

freely choosing one's own fate seems to fly in the face of God's supremacy, and so the common belief is that things have been ordained for every creature.

A STORY OF FAITH

An Iraqi Muslim Sheikh and Jesus

It was May 2001, and I was amazed that God had placed me among the dignitaries of Iraq at a Muslim-Christian dialogue conference in Baghdad initiated by Saddam Hussein. But there I was. Earlier we had toured the country from north to south, seen ancient Babylon and the four-thousand-year-old city of Nineveh, where Jonah preached, and met many wonderful Iraqi people. During the conference, Chaldean and Syriac Christian bishops, patriarchs, and the like talked about their two thousand years of church history. During the closing ceremony at the Saddam Hussein Hall, however, the only non-Christian to speak that day—the leading Muslim Shi'ite cleric in Iraq—was the one who spoke most passionately about Jesus. It was incredible.

He talked directly from John chapter eight, about Jesus and the woman caught in adultery. Two thousand people sat stunned, not so much because a Muslim was speaking about Jesus—that happens—but because he was speaking seemingly with some authority, almost like he knew something more about Jesus than what he was saying. Reading so freely from the Bible was also a bit unusual. When he finished, he walked off the stage and out the back door with his entourage.

Immediately I snuck out the back to see if I could have a word with him. I found him and told him how impressed I was by what he had to say. Then I asked if he would come to Lebanon and spend some time with me and other leaders (mostly Muslim) who were also thinking about and talking about Jesus. His eyes lit up as he said YES! The only problem was that no one could leave Iraq without official permission, and he'd have to get that from a top minister in the government. He gave me the name of the man I needed to ask, someone who possibly was attending the conference. When we exchanged good-byes, the cleric told me, "*Ensha'allah* (God willing) I'll see you in Beirut one day." Frankly, I felt a little foolish for having been so naïve to think it was possible.

With that, I went on a manhunt to find the cabinet member the cleric had mentioned. The next morning I spotted him in the hotel lobby, tightly surrounded by armed bodyguards. After being turned away by two bodyguards, a third one allowed me to speak to the minister, who was wearing an army beret and was decked out in full military regalia.

I stepped up and blurted out, "Hi, my name is Carl. I'm an American who lives in Beirut and I'm here for this conference. I heard your friend the sheikh speak yesterday. He talked about Jesus in a very personal way, and I invited him to Lebanon, but he said I'd need to ask you, and now here you are, so can he come?"

The man seemed shocked by my outburst, but he

quickly looked around and said, "Come over here." We went behind a half wall.

"I'll let him go under one condition."

"Okay, what's that?" I asked.

"Invite me too."

I don't know if you've ever felt so in over your head that it doesn't really matter what you say, but that's how I felt. So I said, "Sure." (All the while thinking, *Since when do I have the authority to invite Iraqi leaders to Lebanon?* but never mind. . . .)

Three months later, they came. The leading Iraqi sheikh and the cabinet minister. They also brought three members of the Iraqi parliament. They stayed in a hotel next to our house in Beirut, and we spent several days reading the Gospels and talking about who Jesus was and is. Amazingly, they had no time to talk about politics. They just wanted Jesus!

For some this may seem surprising. Even incredible. Why would they do this? Were they happy to talk about Jesus from the Bible or just the Qur'an? What things did we talk about from the life of Christ? All good questions. Thanks for asking. . . .

Hopefully you're seeing more and more a central theme to this book: Muslims are happy to talk about matters of faith and about Jesus Christ specifically. Their understanding of him and his work isn't the same as ours, but to engage a Muslim in a serious conversation about Jesus of Nazareth is quite easy. While some Muslims believe today's Bible has been changed from the original text, most are still willing to explore what it has to say about Jesus. I've found that they are typically unwilling to come right out and contradict what the Gospels teach. So I just assume we're all on the same page and move along.

With these men, we had the time to talk about nearly everything. So many people want to know more about what Jesus did and said. His miracles and his teachings. As Christians, we sometimes want to jump ahead to the deeper stuff and get into the doctrines about Jesus, rather than focus on his life itself. But if we're patient, like God has been with us, we can get there. One step at a time.

That's what happened to these men. They were first intrigued, then attracted, and finally overwhelmed by who this man was and what his life meant. That's just part one to each of their journeys!

A CHRISTLIKE PERSPECTIVE

Because Christians believe, as do Muslims, that there is only one God, we have an opportunity to enjoy much shared ground. Notice I said *enjoy*. I did not say *exploit*. It is very critical that you keep in mind how sacred the faith of the Muslim is to him. Do not treat it with disregard.

Having said that, the best advice I can give you is to think before you speak. Because God is holy, and because he is One (at unity with himself), you should stay on that topic. Don't open a can of worms by using a polemic explanation, i.e., starting by trying to explain the concept of the Trinity. There will be time enough for such discussions down the road, but at the beginning of a relationship stick with conversations about the Scriptures, God, and Jesus. Keep in mind the Muslim's perception of the deity of Christ, his sonship, and the cross, and go there when your new Muslim friend is ready and the Holy Spirit is leading. I'm not encouraging you to be wishy-washy about your faith; rather, be sensitive to the Holy Spirit and go at his pace.

To open dialogue, what I find most effective and most Christlike is to stay focused on Jesus. I talk about his leadership style, his wisdom, his teachings, and his miracles. I have sat and prayed with many influential Muslim businessmen and political leaders, and never once have I been chastised for talking about *Isa al-Mesiah*: Jesus the Christ.

When Jesus becomes an object of centrality in anyone, a polarizing effect takes place: The people with whom you are involved will either be uncomfortable, or they will be interested. I'm not saying their current attitude about Jesus is a litmus test of their faith; I believe that Jesus brings all things necessary with himself. And that's why I take *only him* into the relationship.

Muslims are often more interested in angels than Christians are. It's not often that a sore subject comes to the surface regarding angels, but in case it does—once again—be sensitive. You may just want to take it back to the core issue rather than focusing on the disparities of the two faiths.

Feel free to discuss the prophets, theirs and ours. Most, as you've seen, overlap. Muslims enjoy discussing the qualities of the prophets, and there is plenty of room to talk about Moses, Abraham, Jesus, David, and Muhammad. However, a reminder: Don't be irreverent, and if one of your friends challenges you on a point of dispute, don't be defensive. In fact, I've tried to make it a personal goal to *never* argue with my Muslim friends. Whatever their objections may be, I try to nudge the discussion back to the person, works, and words of Jesus of Nazareth.

Know the Qur'an. Read at least some of it. If you don't have a copy, get one. Don't worry if you can't read Arabic; English translations are available. By meeting someone halfway in a discussion about *their* holy book, you will find more freedom in your relationship as well as some gratitude for your openness with them. Although the more fundamental reaches of Islam hold that only the Arabic Qur'an is correct (this is actually Islamic doctrine, that the Qur'an exists in the heavens in Arabic), you will gain miles of respect by showing your sincerity. Despite the Arabic propensity for emotionalism, you will find that most Muslims enjoy an honest conversation.

The English version of the Qur'an that I'd recommend (and the one used for this book) is from Oxford University Press and translated by Abdel Haleem, since Muslims greatly respect that English translation. Some other translations are not particularly easy to read, but don't give up. (Note:

If you are looking up specific verses, know that some verses are inconsistently numbered among the translations, so you might have to search a bit.)

RECOGNIZING STEREOTYPES AND RELIGIOUS "BY-PRODUCTS"

Not only should you try to avoid making stereotypes of Muslims, you should try to avoid reinforcing stereotypes of Christians.

For centuries, many people have reduced the conflict to a simplistic generalization, *Christianity vs. Islam.* So using harmful terminology, or making distinctions about who did what and who's right and who's not, and all of that other stuff, will just put you in a bind. Guaranteed. It will also make you defensive, which misses the entire point. One example: I learned a long time ago that thinking of myself as a Christian missionary was the quickest way to lose the interest of new friends, let alone an audience. I simply tell people that I'm a follower of Jesus, and usually, with a little explanation, things aren't so guarded and tense. Jesus doesn't come loaded with bias, prejudice, conflict, or war. Christianity often does.

In the Western court of opinion, the concept of Islam typically conveys images of *mujahedin* (guerrilla warriors) in black robes with AK-47s and scimitars (curved sabers) sweeping through the desert on nomadic raids and pillaging tents. We have this idea in the West that Muslims are loose-cannon radicals with destruction in mind and automatic weapons in hand.

While it's true that some terrorists utilize the banner of Islam to kill and destroy, the majority of Muslims are far more concerned with obeying the commandments of God, and many already live so close to the truths of Jesus that they're within reach of their hearts.

If we were to compare religions side-by-side in terms of actual behavior, you would see that many Muslims are actually more "religious" (in practical terms, i.e., prayers, traditions, and duties) than many Christians. This devotion is typical for Arabs and is a part of their temperament. It is Islam—submission to God.

People often make blanket statements like, "Those Muslims..." or, "Why can't Islam stop the fighting?" The problem is that such statements equate the sins of an individual to the fault of the whole, when this simply is not the case. There is a key distinction between the vast majority of Muslims (who want peace and prosperity, like you and I do) and the extremists (who believe that all people, including other Muslims, are condemned).

I have many friends who are Catholic and if, during the seventies and eighties, people were to have broadly blamed Catholicism for the terrorism in Belfast, they would have been completely wrong. Everybody knows Catholics are not terrorists. Neither are Muslims. Terrorists are terrorists.

Like all religions, Islam has developed many traditions or "by-products." These have come about as a result of fourteen hundred years of practicing Islam. Often, these by-products are what the Western world perceives to be Islam itself.

The foremost is the concept of *jihad*. The word literally means "struggle" in Arabic, and it was conceptually, in origin, the idea of religious struggle, much like the early church after the ascension of Christ. However, there is no doubt about the primary meaning associated with jihad today: holy war.

The headlines and casualties of terrorism are the first things we think of when we hear the word *jihad*. This is, without a doubt, a by-product of the military campaigns of Muhammad, and in recent times, the global struggle of some Muslims to resurrect the historical power of Islam to create an international community with a legitimate and recognized caliphate (Muslim form of government). Still, I must say that of the thousands of Muslims I'm acquainted with and the hundreds who I'd consider friends, and in the many Muslim countries I've traveled in, I've never met a Muslim who believes that Islam should conquer the world by the sword.

Another by-product or tradition associated with Islam is seen in some places in the world where Muslims maintain a definite anti-modern approach to life. This could be an outgrowth of Muhammad's original intent to return his countrymen back to the old ways and the one true God. In fact, there is a sense among these nations that the contemporary West has fallen by the moral wayside as shown by its media, domestic violence and divorce rates, and materialism.

Additionally, the culture at the time of Islam's inception was tribal. Leadership was based on eldership. Nation-states were ruled by a monarch whose brothers and cousins all formed the top of a social caste system. Today this can be seen in the tendency of Islamic states to rule by direct dictatorship. Even Iraq, which was until lately a secular state under the rule of Saddam Hussein, was a dictatorship governing (or suppressing) various factions and sects, primarily the Kurdish north and the Shi'ite south.

Due to the strong tribal aspects of most Muslim countries, as well as Muslims' high view of authority and sovereignty, democracy is often a difficult proposition. Iraq is an obvious case in point. The entire concept of representative government does not gel with strong religious leadership, much of which comes directly from the Muslim concept of God. God is not elected, he simply *is,* and his authority is unquestionable. The ideology of individualism, which we so value in the West and which leads more naturally into a democratic society, is virtually nonexistent in the Islamic world.

Muslim immigrants living in the U.S. are a diverse group, as you might guess. Many came to the States to either escape an uncomfortable living situation or to generally better their life—like any other immigrant. Because of their strong familial identification, many Muslims will move to places where they can stay in their sub-groups. In Dearborn, Michigan, for instance, you'll find Arabs living together. But not just Arabs in general: Yemeni Arabs in one area and Lebanese Arabs in another.

Freedom, democracy, and capitalism all tug firmly on the head, heart, and wallet of any Muslim, even though many of their home countries don't see any of these things as being in line with their particular version of Islam.

If you've traveled outside the U.S., you've seen the love-hate relationship much of the world has with America. Our country's stability, open society, and opportunities to "make it big" are a strong draw. The Marlboro Man, Will Smith, and Madonna round out much of what the world sees us as offering. But it's those very same elements that create an invincible aura around America and play a part in her international reputation. Many people just feel overwhelmed by all things American. It's no wonder, then, that Muslims more than most—with all of their inbuilt sensitivities to the above—would be skeptical and suspicious of the exporter of such things, even as the draw to Lady Liberty in the New York harbor remains strong.

Finally, another by-product of Islam is the concept of *maktub*, or what we could arguably call fatalism. Muslim friends have explained to me that it means simply "as God wills it," or "such is my lot," or even, "it has been decided upon."

For the Muslim, God has a clearly predetermined will, and he acts upon it without question. Therefore, the Muslim does not question it either, even if it does not make sense.

One of my good friends, an American Air Force pilot, once told me that he'd flown on training sorties with his pilot equivalents in Saudi Arabia. At one time, while flying with a Saudi pilot, during an equipment malfunction, the jet appeared to be on a direct collision course with the terrain. While my friend busied himself with emergency procedures, he noticed that his Saudi counterpart was seated calmly with his hands in his lap, putting no effort into changing their course.

"What are you doing?" my friend shouted. "We're going to crash!"

"If so," replied the Saudi pilot, "it is as Allah wills."

THE FIVE PILLARS

The structure of Islam is based upon five pillars of religion—five basic tenets—that Muslims are required to observe: the testimony, the fast, giving, prayer, and a pilgrimage to Mecca. For a handful of small fundamentalist sects, there is a sixth pillar I've already mentioned: jihad, or holy war. But very few Muslims would agree with jihad as a sixth pillar. We'll address this issue in detail in chapter 6.

These five pillars are clearly expressed within the Qur'an itself, and you will find that those who are devoted to them are exemplary people who may not feel or even appear as though they are in need of more, or a different, religion. This is, in fact, true. Jesus is what they (and we) need. Not another religion!

The pillars of faith could be best compared to the tenets of Judaism or to the Christian doctrines; they're not the same in substance, but they follow the same form as the other classical religions. The pillars are guidelines for faith, and in Islamic states they are law, which is either obeyed or enforced. Those who live outside of these tenets, if they are allowed to maintain their own faith, are typically required to pay *zakat*, a form of taxation.

The pillars are regarded as necessary in the majority of the Muslim world. They are similar in many ways to Jewish Law in that they are mandated, and to disregard them is to sin against God.

Islam is based largely on works. As in many religions, there is not always a passion for genuine spirituality, but rather a fear of God's wrath and the consequences of angering him. I am often aware of a very heavy sense of works-related religiosity. In Sunni mosques (we'll get into the distinctions between Muslim sects in chapter 6), balance scales are depicted on the walls to represent how God ultimately will judge each person by his deeds, prayer mats are on the floor, and every space is pervaded with a sense of devotion that seems to be borne of equal parts anxiety and desire.

We Christians also have prophets of law, though, and that law can guide us (and Muslims) to the grace and truth of Jesus Christ.

Now, on to the elements practiced by the vast majority of Muslims in one form or another—the five pillars of Islam.

1. The Testimony (*Shahadah*). *There is no god but God, and Muhammad is the prophet of God.* This is a confession of belief in God. This is the basic and first step of Islam, to say with your mouth and believe in your heart that there is only one true God, and that Muhammad is his final messenger. To many Muslims, this alone makes you a Muslim. Obviously, Christians can and do agree with the first (but not the second) part of this statement. There *is* no god but God. On many occasions I have been welcomed into a Muslim home because I simply agreed that there is no god but God.

2. The Fast (*Sawm*, observed primarily during *Ramadan*, the ninth month of the Muslim lunar calendar). According to tradition, Ramadan is a month-long fast to commemorate the revelations given from God through Gabriel to Muhammad. Muslims are required to observe a dawn-to-dusk fast from food, drink, tobacco, and other items. After sunset, a meal to break the fast (*iftar*) is eaten, and prayer is invoked for forgiveness of sins already committed and sins not yet committed.

In some of the nations under the rule of Islamic Law (*Sharia*), there are very strict enforcements regulated for those who trespass the fast of Ramadan, and the consequences can be harsh.

3. Giving (*Zakat*). This varies in each country, and also by class and income, but by and large, each Muslim is required to give at least 2.5% of his or her assets to the poor. The poor could be defined as the sick, travelers, or even new converts to Islam. During my years in the Middle East, I have been befriended by numerous Muslims, some of whom were people of means. What I noticed right away was their propensity to give upon request. One, a wealthy businessman, employs a supervisor to oversee his *voluntary* almsgivings; meaning that my friend does not only give his required percentage, but he donates, based upon need, out of compassion.

Despite the fact that giving is obligatory, many Muslims do give out of compassion. This is one of the greatest paths of friendship you can have with a Muslim. I used to meet regularly with political and business leaders in Lebanon (even leaders in Hamas and Hezballah) in order to pray for the refugees and the poor. The center of every discussion was compassion: how we could ease suffering, open schools, and provide medical attention. This is key: Jesus is exemplified by compassion. He can be a primary discussion point when you are conversing with a devout Muslim about suffering and compassion.

Muslims are typically people of honor, and a portion of that honor is found in the readiness of compassion. This, in my estimation, is often above the 2.5% standard set by the commandments.

4. Prayer (*Salat*). As you may know, Muslims are required to pray at certain times each day: at sunrise, shortly after noon, midafternoon, after sundown, and after nightfall.

Only the most serious Muslims actually stop and pray five times a day. As is the case with many people in any religion, prayer often becomes a mere ritual and is sometimes relegated to the holy day, which, in Islam, is Friday.

Daily prayers of Islam are conveyed in ritual format. If you were in the Middle East, you'd hear a call to prayer chanted from the minaret of the mosque. The mosque often uses amplification so that the people in the outlying areas can be prepared for prayer as well. The nearby Muslims respond to the *azan* (the call), and the prayer commences with a series of statements and responses.

Muslims face toward Mecca when they pray. Every mosque has a marker designating the proper direction, and most Muslims always know which direction is correct—even if they're indoors.

Tradition holds that Muslims have always prayed in the direction of Mecca because it is the birthplace of the prophet. However, most historians now agree that for a short time, in the beginning, they prayed in the direction of Jerusalem, the city of David and Jesus. Due to some conflict with the Jews in Medina, the original followers decided to pray a little further to the southeast, toward the city of Muhammad's birth.

The posture of prayer is important to all sects and varieties of Muslims. The forehead must contact the ground, and some Muslims wear a long robe so that they can remove their shoes and retain a sense of modesty. Of course, many Muslims don't wear a robe at all; they wear some kind of pants or trousers. You will seldom see a Muslim man wearing shorts, as it's considered immodest.

All Muslims remove their shoes in order to respect what is holy during prayer.

Each time before prayer the feet are washed, as are the hands and forearms, as a ritual cleansing. It is commonly believed that a clean outside reflects a clean inside, and you will note that most Muslims are extremely clean and tidy.

The prayers are recitations, and they are pronounced in sets and intervals. Each individual responds in confession of God's greatness, acknowledgment of his wisdom, and a plea for mercy. The steps are followed with a prostrated bow, in acceptance of and submission to God's greatness.

If ever you have an opportunity to observe Muslim prayers, it's a worthwhile experience. If you are polite, respectful, and courteous you may gain a friend, and you may well find yourself in the privileged position to learn a few things—both in your relationship with your Muslim friend and in your relationship with God.

5. Pilgrimage (*Hajj*). All Muslims who are able are required to make a journey to Mecca. The capability of travel, by tradition, has been the means to afford the journey, as well as the physical ability to travel. Some allow a pilgrimage by proxy, and there are concessions for those who are ill or otherwise unable to make the trip during their lifetime.

Only Muslims can go into the Kaaba shrine, also called "the house." No outsider has had any claim to having seen the black stone that "fell from heaven." Muslims are encouraged to kiss this black stone, which, according to tradition, was once white but has been turned black by the touch of some sinful men. If the crowd is too thick, they must touch it with a hand or a walking stick.

After visiting the Kaaba, most Muslims visit other places in Saudi Arabia, including Mt. Arafat as well as Mina, to throw stones at a series of three pillars, one of which is thought to represent the devil. Finally, there is a visitation to the tomb of Muhammad at Medina. Over two million people participate in the annual pilgrimage to Saudi Arabia.

A CHRISTLIKE PERSPECTIVE

Know these five pillars. They help build bridges. If you sincerely want to develop friendships with Muslims, you need areas of common interest, and it would behoove you to know what it is that they believe and are obligated to do.

Don't attempt to argue with the testimony. In truth, the testimony is correct in that there *is* only one God, and his name, in Arabic, *is* Allah. In fact, from the day of Pentecost, when Arabs first believed (see Acts 2:11), Arabs have been calling God "Allah." (How English speakers began calling God "God" is another interesting story for another book.) As far as Muhammad goes, be careful. I understand that our desire will be strong to confront the issue of who Muhammad was because we believe he *wasn't* a prophet, but I'd recommend changing the subject, because this topic is not open to debate for your Muslim friend. It will take a revelation from the Holy Spirit before this is up for discussion. (At that time, discuss away.)

Muhammad said many things that *are* true, particularly some of his teachings about Jesus. Whether or not God holds him as a prophet won't be a productive discussion point because his followers believe that he was, and it doesn't hurt our testimony to allow them that. Remember to stick to our goal—live and speak Jesus.

Muhammad taught that Jesus was born of a virgin (Q 19:20), worked miracles (Q 3:49; 5:110), had no sin (Q 19:19), and was the Word of God (Q 4:171), and he even went so far as to call him "Jesus the Christ" (Q 3:45).

Since the above points from the Qur'an are true, we don't need to worry about where they came from, as all truth is God's truth. Let's rejoice that God has many ways to convey that truth and even other traditions and religions can incorporate some truth that ultimately comes from God.

HOW TO RESPECT THE FIVE PILLARS

Regarding the fast, it's pretty simple: Don't eat in front of any of your Muslim friends during Ramadan.

Be careful not to walk in front of a praying Muslim.
Go around, or wait.

When praying yourself, stand, kneel, or hold out your

hands with the palms upward. Let your Muslim friends know that you pray (without being a hypocrite). Muslims often think that Christians don't pray, because they don't see us publicly praying as they do.

Honor the almsgiving. *In fact, participate when you can. As always, you should be quick to regard what is virtuous, and you should not take it upon yourself to point out what is not. Humbly share with them the times you give tithes and offerings, while sharing your motivation for doing so.*

Lastly, realize that for every Muslim practice, Jesus has said something that is relevant. *Because the teachings of Jesus are important to your Muslim friends, you have all the conversational material you need. (I list the main Qur'anic verses about Jesus in the next chapter.)*

CHAPTER 3

Islam's Holy Book: What the Qur'an Says About Jesus

Of all the elements of Islam, I can think of none more in need of discussion than the Muslim holy book, the Qur'an. It is important to take an honest look at what is taught in the Qur'an, what our Muslim friends believe, and how as friends and as followers of Jesus we can interface with them.

This can be difficult at first because of the amount of bias against and misinformation about Islam and its followers. It is with the same bias that some people approach a discussion about the holiest book of Islam, the Qur'an.

Just as there are wrong ideas about Islam, there are misperceptions about its holy book. In fact, the Qur'an is quite possibly the greatest inroad we have to reach the hearts of our Muslim friends. Having said that, I must also say that some things in the Qur'an *are* confusing, even contradictory. A handful of verses do condone killing, and other verses, depending on how they're interpreted, deny things we know to be true. Most notably, the Qur'an disputes the crucifixion, citing that it was not Jesus on the cross (although this too is open to various interpretations). Despite these theological differences, there is a gold mine running through the Qur'an: His name is Jesus (Isa). The Qur'an mentions Jesus almost one hundred times, all with great reverence.

As we learn more about Islam and the Qur'an, we must begin by asking Jesus to give us his attitude. The Holy Spirit will give us, if we ask him, a way to love Muslims without prejudices. Prejudice will find a way to taint and disease our relationships with our Muslim friends, and it could even distort what we say about Jesus.

In his excellent book *Building Bridges,* the late pastor Fouad Elias Accad, of Lebanon, gave a fitting example of how bias can affect relationships.

> Suppose a man who had shaved off all his hair and
> who wrapped himself in a bright orange sarong
> came into my community proclaiming "God's
> Truth." No matter how sincere and loving he was, I
> would be dead set against renouncing my culture to

accept his "truth" about God and becoming like him. But, if he had behaved according to the ways of my culture, and treated my beliefs with respect, it would be far easier to hear what he was saying and to seriously consider it.[1]

Obviously, we don't have to convert to Islam in order to reach Muslims, but being conscientious about the history of conflict between Islam and Christianity, and doing our best to stay open-minded, will give us a lot more mileage than disputing the Qur'an from the start with an argumentative or apologetic approach.

THE HISTORY OF THE QUR'AN

Muhammad was not (at least early in his career) building a religion to displace Judaism and Christianity. The vast majority of his teachings were along the same lines as the two other monotheistic religions. In fact, Muhammad viewed his teachings to be "more of the same," simply directed to his Arab countrymen. For possibly six hundred years after the time of Christ, there were no Arabic translations of Jewish or Christian prophecies, teachings, or holy books. Still, it is known that Muhammad felt an obligation to turn his countrymen away from idolatry and back to the ways of "the people of the book" (Christians and Jews).

---

[1] Fouad Elias Accad, *Building Bridges: Christianity and Islam* (Colorado Springs: Nav-Press), 34.

Muslims believe that during the last twenty years of Muhammad's life, he was given messages from God in installments. The Qur'an is the perfect and unimpeachable recording of God's words, which came down in full and intact to Muhammad. According to Muslim belief, the Qur'an exists eternally in heaven in the form of tablets, and the angel Gabriel helped Muhammad collect these revelations, word for word from the stone tablets in heaven, which are also in Arabic.

Muhammad verbally transmitted these revelations, but there was no complete Qur'an written at the time of his death in 632. As time went on, different individuals wrote down the teachings, and there was some variation between scripts, though perhaps not significant variances. It wasn't until the year 652 that there was an "official" version of the Qur'an, which rendered all others obsolete.

Fragments of early Qur'anic scripts have been found, dating back to the eighth century. Interestingly, the script excluded punctuation and vowels, which, according to some, makes for a transcription that could be translated a number of ways.

THE QUR'AN AND THE BIBLE

One thing to be careful to observe is that Muslims do not associate the Qur'an and its writings with any human authors, as we do with various books of the Bible (the books of James, Peter, Jude, etc.). Again, Islamic tradition holds that the Qur'an comes directly from God—that he is the one speaking. It is blasphemous to attribute the Qur'an even to Muhammad.

Many Muslims consider the Bible to be a holy book, but they are reluctant to read it because they think the Qur'an says that early Christians and Jews changed the original wording. However, this is one example of how many Muslims are not very knowledgeable about the Qur'an. It does not say the Bible has been changed, though it has become commonplace to believe it has been changed anyway.

The Qur'an is organized into 114 *surahs*, or chapters. Some surahs are lengthy; some very short ones have just a few verses in all. They are arranged in order of length, with the longer surahs in the beginning and the shorter ones at the end (with the notable exception of surah 1, which is short). Each surah has a title. For instance, *Yusuf* is the twelfth surah, the story of Joseph; and *Maryam* is the nineteenth surah, the story of Mary and the birth of Jesus. Some of them are poetic, like our Psalms. Others deal more with the concrete issues of life and the practical aspects of religion.

The verses themselves are called *ayas*, or *ayat*. The Arabic word *aya* is best translated as "sign" or "miracle."

As a tool to help Christians understand and relate to Muslims, I've organized a list of verses from the Qur'an and summarized what they say about Jesus. Also provided are correlating verses from the New Testament. I am not suggesting the Bible verses say the same thing as the Qur'an. They are provided simply as points of reference. I encourage you to pick up a copy of the Qur'an and do some homework in finding topics you'd like to discuss with a Muslim. As mentioned earlier, in Muslim circles the Abdel Haleem translation is a well respected English version of the Qur'an.

For reference, the first number listed is the number of the surah (chapter), which is done with Roman numerals in the English translation, and the second number is the ayat (verse). So, Q 3:53 means surah III, ayat 53.

WHAT THE QUR'AN SAYS ABOUT . . .

THE CONCEPTION AND BIRTH OF JESUS:

- GOD FOREORDAINED THE BIRTH OF JESUS (ISA)—Q 3:47 (Matthew 1:23)

- GOD COMMANDED JESUS' BIRTH—Q 3:47 (Luke 1:31, 35)

- JESUS' BIRTH WAS A MIRACLE TO MANKIND—Q 21:91 (Luke 2:8–20; Matthew 2:1–12)

- THE DAY OF JESUS' BIRTH WAS BLESSED—Q 19:33 (Luke 2:10–14)

- JESUS IS THE SON OF MARY (MARYAM)—Q 3:36; Q 3:45 (Luke 2:7; Matthew 13:55)

- JESUS CONFIRMS HIS OWN LEGITIMACY (IN THE CRADLE)— Q 19:29 (Matthew 1:18–25)

- NO MAN HAD TOUCHED MARY WHEN SHE BECAME PREGNANT WITH JESUS—Q 19:20; Q 21:91 (Matthew 1:18)

- GOD SENT HIS SPIRIT TO MARY AND IT TOOK THE FORM OF A MAN—Q 19:27 (Luke 1:26–35)

- GOD SENT HIS SPIRIT TO GIVE MARY A SINLESS SON—Q 19:19; Q 66:12 (Luke 1:35)

- JESUS WAS SENT DOWN FROM HEAVEN—Q 3:53 (Philippians 2:5–8)

- GOD CREATED JESUS—Q 3:47, BUT ALSO SEE Q 21:91 (Matthew 1:18–20)

THE CHARACTER OF JESUS:

- GOD MADE JESUS AN EXAMPLE TO THE PEOPLE OF ISRAEL—Q 43:49 (1 Timothy 18–20)

- GOD COMMANDED JESUS TO HONOR HIS MOTHER—Q 19:32 (John 19:26)

- GOD DID NOT MAKE JESUS PROUD OR REBELLIOUS—Q 19:32 (Mark 7:36)

- JESUS IS RIGHTEOUS—Q 3:46; Q 6:85 (John 8:46)

- JESUS ONLY DID WHAT GOD TOLD HIM TO DO—Q 5:117 (John 14:1, 10)

THE DEATH OF JESUS:

- PEOPLE PLOTTED AGAINST JESUS—Q 3:54 (John 12:10)

- GOD CAN DO ANYTHING HE WANTS TO—EVEN ALLOW JESUS TO DIE—Q 5:17 (Luke 1:37)

- GOD SAID TO JESUS THAT HE WOULD MAKE HIM DIE—Q 3:55 (Mark 14:36)

- WHEN GOD MADE CHRIST DIE, GOD HIMSELF BECAME THE OVERSEER—Q 5:117 (John 17:14)

- ·JESUS WAS ONE OF THE MESSENGERS WHO WAS KILLED BY ISRAEL—Q 2:87; Q 5:70 (Acts 7:52; Luke 11:49)

- ·THE JEWS KILLED JESUS AND OTHER PROPHETS—Q 2:91 (Acts 2:36; 3:15; 4:10; 5:30)

- ·THE JEWS THEMSELVES *DID NOT* KILL OR CRUCIFY CHRIST— Q 4:157 (Luke 23:24–25)

- THE ONES WHO KILLED CHRIST WEREN'T REALLY THE KILL-ERS, BECAUSE IT WAS GOD'S PLAN—Q 8:17, BUT ALSO SEE Q 4:157, 158 (Acts 2:23)

- CHRIST WAS DEAD AND GOD RAISED HIM—Q 6:122 (Romans 6:4–11)

- THE DAY JESUS DIED WAS BLESSED—Q 19:33 (Luke 2:10–14)

JESUS BEING EXALTED:

- JESUS IS THE KNOWLEDGE OF THE LAST DAYS—Q 43:61 (Luke 21:25–28; 17:30)

- THE KNOWLEDGE OF THE LAST DAYS IS GOD'S—Q 41:47; Q 43:61 (Matthew 24:36)

- GOD AIDED JESUS WITH THE HOLY SPIRIT—Q 2:87; Q 2:253; Q 5:110 (1 Peter 1:2; Matthew 4:1; 12:18; Luke 4:18)

- OHN THE BAPTIST (YAHYA) TESTIFIED OF JESUS—Q 3:39 (John 1:29–34)

- GOD PREFERRED JESUS ABOVE THE OTHER MESSENGERS— Q 2:253 (Hebrews 1:1–3; Matthew 21:33–41)

- JESUS PRONOUNCED PEACE UPON HIMSELF—Q 19:33 (John 13:13–17)

- JESUS INTERCEDES WITH GOD ACCORDING TO GOD'S WILL— Q 2:255 (1 Timothy 2:5; Hebrews 7:25; Romans 8:27, 34)

- GOD EXALTED JESUS—Q 2:253 (Philippians 2:9)

- JESUS IS DISTINGUISHED IN THE WORLD—Q 3:45 (John 5:22)

- JESUS IS NEAR TO GOD—Q 3:45 (JOHN 14:7–9)

- JESUS IS BLESSED—Q 43:61, SEE ALSO Q 43:85 (Matthew 21:9)

- GOD MADE JESUS BLESSED WHEREVER HE WENT—Q 19:31 (Mark 7:37)

- GOD MADE A COVENANT WITH HIS PROPHETS (INCLUDING JESUS)—
Q 33:7 (Luke 4:18, 43)

THE FOLLOWERS OF JESUS:

- GOD'S HELPERS ARE THOSE WHO HELP JESUS—Q 3:52; Q 61:14 (1 John 2:23)

- JESUS HAD FOLLOWERS—Q 3:53 (John 3:26)

- GOD SAID TO JESUS THAT HE WOULD MAKE HIS FOLLOWERS HIGHER THAN THE UNBELIEVERS UNTIL JUDGMENT DAY— Q 3:55 (Ephesians 2:6)

- JESUS TOLD GOD THAT THE DISCIPLES WERE GOD'S SERVANTS, AND HE COULD CHOOSE TO TORTURE OR FORGIVE THEM—Q 5:118 (John 17:6–11)

- THE CHRISTIANS SAY THAT JESUS (MESSIAH) IS THE SON OF GOD (ALLAH)—Q 9:30 (John 20:30–31)

- THE CHRISTIANS TOOK JESUS THE SON OF MARY AS LORD INSTEAD OF GOD—Q 9:31 (1 Corinthians 8:6)

JESUS AS THE FULFILLMENT:

- JESUS CONFIRMED THE OLD TESTAMENT THAT WAS IN HIS HANDS—Q 3:50; Q 5:46 (Luke 4:21; 16:17; Matthew 5:18; 15:1–6)

THE HUMANITY OF JESUS:

- JESUS ATE FOOD—Q 5:75 (Luke 24:43)

- JESUS SPOKE TO THE PEOPLE WHEN AN ADULT—Q 3:46;
  Q 5:110 (Matthew 5–7; John 14:10)

- GOD GAVE JESUS REFUGE—Q 23:50 (Luke 4:30)

- GOD IS JESUS' LORD—Q 5:117 (Philippians 1:3)

- GOD GAVE COMMANDMENTS TO JESUS—Q 42:13
  (Hebrews 1:5, 8, 12–13)

- GOD COMMANDED JESUS TO PRAY AND GIVE ALMS WHILE HE
  REMAINED ALIVE (ON EARTH)—Q 19:31
  (John 17:1–6; 13:29; Luke 6:12; Matthew 19:21)

JESUS AND JUDGMENT DAY:

- ON JUDGMENT DAY, JESUS WILL WITNESS AGAINST THOSE
  WHO DID NOT BELIEVE IN HIM BEFORE THEIR DEATH—
  Q 4:159 (John 5:22–23)

JESUS AND HIS MIRACLES:

- THE CHILD JESUS CREATED A CLAY BIRD FOR THE JEWS AND
  BREATHED LIFE INTO IT—Q 3:49; Q 5:110 (John 5:21; 20:22)

- JESUS GAVE SIGHT TO A MAN BORN BLIND—Q 3:49; Q 5:110
  (John 9:1–12)

- JESUS HEALED A LEPER, RAISED THE DEAD, AND PROPHE-
  SIED—Q 3:49; Q 5:110
  (John 6:47–49; 11:43–44; Mark 12:40)

- CHRIST ASKED GOD TO PROVIDE A MEAL FROM HEAVEN—
  Q 5:112–114 (John 6:5–14)

- GOD GAVE MIRACLES TO JESUS—Q 2:87, 253 (John 6:11–14)

- JESUS CAME WITH MIRACLES—Q 43:63; Q 61:16
  (Matthew 12:22–32)

THE NAMES OF JESUS:

- *CHRIST* IS JESUS' TITLE—Q 4:157, 171 (John 4:25)
- HIS NAME IS *MESSIAH*, JESUS, SON OF MARY—Q 3:45
  (Matthew 1:21)
- JESUS IS A SPIRIT FROM GOD—Q 4:171 (Luke 1:35)
- JESUS IS A MERCY FROM GOD—Q 19:21 (Acts 2:23)
- JESUS WAS A MIRACLE TO ALL MEN—Q 21:91 (Luke 2:8–20)
- CHRIST WAS A WITNESS OVER THE PEOPLE WHILE WITH
  THEM—Q 5:117 (John 17:12–13)

JESUS AS A PROPHET:

- GOD AIDED JESUS WITH THE HOLY SPIRIT—Q 2:87, 253;
  Q 5:110 (1 Peter 1:2; Matthew 4:1, 12; Luke 4:18)
- GOD CAUSED JESUS TO FOLLOW IN THE LINEAGE OF JEWISH
  PROPHETS—Q 5:46 (Matthew 21:33–41)
- JESUS WAS A PROPHET—Q 2:91 (Luke 11:49)
- JESUS TOLD THE PEOPLE OF ISRAEL THAT A PROPHET WAS
  COMING TO THEM WHOSE NAME WAS PRAISED—Q 61:6 (John
  14:16; 17)

JESUS' RELATIONSHIP TO GOD:

- GOD IS *NOT* CHRIST THE SON OF MARY—Q 5:17, 72
  (1 Corinthians 8:6)
- JESUS IS A SPIRIT FROM GOD—Q 4:171 (Luke 1:35)
- GOD ASKED JESUS IF HE HAD TOLD PEOPLE TO REGARD

HIMSELF AND MARY AS TWO GODS IN PLACE OF GOD—
Q 5:116 (John 10:30; 17:21; Matthew 17:5)

- JESUS ANSWERED THAT HE NEVER SAID ANYTHING HE HAD
  NO RIGHT TO SAY—Q 5:116 (John 14:10)

- GOD COMMANDED JESUS TO HONOR HIS MOTHER—Q 19:32
  (John 19:26)

THE RESURRECTION OF JESUS:

- GOD RAISED JESUS TO HIMSELF—Q 4:158 (Mark 16:19)

- GOD PLOTTED AGAINST THE PEOPLE'S PLOT AND WON—
  Q 3:54 (Revelation 13:8; Matthew 20:17–19; Acts 3:15; 4:10;
  Romans 8:37)

- THE DAY THAT JESUS WAS RAISED WAS BLESSED—Q 19:33
  (Luke 2:10–14)

- GOD SAID TO JESUS THAT HE WOULD RAISE HIM UP ALIVE—
  Q 3:55 (Acts 1:9; Luke 18:33)

JESUS AND REVELATIONS:

- GOD GAVE JESUS THE BIBLE—Q 19:30 (Luke 4:16–20)

- GOD REVEALED TO THE DISCIPLES OF JESUS THAT THEY
  WERE TO BELIEVE IN GOD AND IN HIS MESSENGER, JESUS—
  Q 5:111 (John 6:68–69)

- GOD GAVE JESUS THE NEW TESTAMENT, IN WHICH IS GUID-
  ANCE AND LIGHT—Q 5:46 (Luke 2:32)

- GOD TAUGHT JESUS THE BIBLE AND WISDOM—Q 3:48;
  Q 5:110 (Luke 2:40)

- JESUS IS GREATER THAN THE LAW—Q 3:50 (Mark 7:14–20)

- CHRIST SAID THAT HE BROUGHT THE PEOPLE WISDOM—
  Q 43:63 (Matthew 13:1–52)

JESUS AND SERVANTHOOD:

- JESUS SAID THAT HE WAS GOD'S SERVANT—Q 19:30
  (John 20:17; Philippians 2:5–7)

- JESUS WAS NOT TOO ARROGANT TO BE GOD'S SERVANT—
  Q 4:172 (Philippians 2:6–7)

- JESUS IS ONLY A SERVANT TO WHOM GOD GAVE GRACE—
  Q 43:59, SEE ALSO Q 4:171 (Philippians 2:5–11)

JESUS BEING SINLESS:

- CHRIST IS SINLESS—Q 19:19
  (Hebrews 7:26; 2 Corinthians 5:21; John 8:46)

JESUS AS THE WORD:

- JESUS IS A SAYING OF THE TRUTH—Q 19:34
  (1 John 5:7–12, 20; 2:21; 1:1; 2 John 1)

- JESUS IS A WORD FROM GOD—Q 3:39, 45 (John 1:14)

- JESUS IS GOD'S WORD—Q 4:171 (John 1:1–3)

- GOD SPOKE/CAST HIS WORD TO MARY—Q 4:171
  (Luke 1:35; John 1:14)

A STORY OF FAITH

Snakes, Bibles, and the Hotel Staff

I was sitting in a hotel lobby in a small, southern Iraqi town, rubbing my eyes after a short nap, when three young staff members walked over from the front desk and sat down. They were curious about me and my friends, who had left me to rest. "What are you doing in

Iraq?" asked one of the guys. "Aren't you Americans? My friend says you are Christians."

"Yes, most of us are Americans," I answered, "but we live here in the Middle East. What do you mean when you think we might be Christian?"

"You know," he said, "Christians! People who believe in Israel and the Trinity, and don't like us." He said this without a hesitation, and unfortunately, it is a common opinion.

I had already learned not to defend all of Christendom—the good or the bad—so I said, "Well, I can't speak for others, but I'd love to tell you who we really are." They were hooked (and obviously bored in their jobs) and pulled an overstuffed sofa closer to hear my story.

"We are people of faith. Like you. People who believe in the one true God. Like you. People who want to love their wives and children and do good. Like you. We take prayer seriously. We want to be godly and act justly. Like you."

(A quick note: A great way to treat people in general is to assume that it's *you* who will learn from *them*. Say things that call them to a higher place. Don't belittle. Don't put yourself ahead of them. Don't be condescending. Treat them as you'd like to be treated.)

I continued: "We also try to follow the ways, teachings, and life of Jesus the Messiah. He's our model for all we do and think and say. We're not very good at it, but this is our goal. So we've come here looking to find out if Jesus is here already and what he might want us to do here."

They clearly loved what I was saying and asked for a story about Jesus. My Arabic is not very good, but I began to share the story Jesus told about the prodigal son. Everything was going great until I got to the part where the son returns home. In the Lebanese dialect I learned, the words for *village* and *snake* are very similar (at least to my foreign ears). So what they heard me say was, "As the boy approached his snake . . ." They gasped and, with worried looks, interrupted me to ask if he got bit.

It took me a moment to realize my mistake, but I corrected myself and tried to continue. Still, they wanted to know about the snake. "There's never been a snake in this story. It's a village," I responded, depleted of my original brilliant storytelling capacity. "No snake." They were confused but allowed me to finish what I consider one of Jesus' best stories. It says so much: the hurt, offended father waiting for his son; the father throwing a party and seemingly forgetting the offense; the boy repenting and coming to his senses; the juxtaposition between son and slave; the older son pouting. It's all there. Amazing drama side-by-side with deep theological teaching.

The points of the story hit home. I could sense the presence of the Holy Spirit. God was in that lobby.

Just then, one of the young guys spoke up. "When I was ten, a German man gave my daddy a cassette of stories of Jesus. We gathered at our table and listened to that cassette every night for almost a year. Then it broke. The German man had told my father that Jesus had a book out, but he didn't have one to give us. He told us to look for it and someday we'd get one. Do you know about the book Jesus has?"

I could barely respond at first, but managed to say, "Yes, Jesus does have a book."

"But do you have one?" the young man said with desperation.

"Actually, I have one in my room. Can I get it for you?"

I nearly tripped on the way since I couldn't see through my tears. Thankfully, I had one gospel of Luke left. I brought it out and handed it to him. His eyes widened as he clutched the copy and read the title.

"Is this the real gospel of Jesus Christ?"

"Yes, it's the real one, written by one of his early followers, Luke. You'll love it."

He burst into tears, put it to his forehead, and then kissed it. Next, he surprised us all by running toward the front door. He yelled back, "I have to go show my father. He'll be so excited!"

Wow! The other guys turned to me and almost fell over themselves asking if I had more books. It was my last copy, I said, but I promised them books too.

We were still talking when the young man returned, out of breath. "I showed it to my father and uncles and they all agreed it is the true book of Jesus. But they said I had to get more for other family members and friends. Please, do you have more?"

This is a common response to the Bible in the Muslim world. It contains the very words of God, and when we treat them as such, people will be hungry for them. Who wouldn't want to read what God has written to us?

A CHRISTLIKE PERSPECTIVE

Of critical importance to the follower of Jesus who wishes to befriend a Muslim is knowing the religious, political, and cultural barriers. Islam is not merely a different society—a different clique of individuals—but also a vastly different culture. The barriers might be lower with Muslims living in the United States and other Western countries, but in conversations you can still feel as though you are talking to someone from another planet. That is the way the world is—the East and the West have always been different, and God willing, they always will be, to some degree.

The first step is to make it a personal journey with Jesus at the helm. By being sensitive, using your instincts within the relationship, and trusting the guidance of the Holy Spirit, you have all the things necessary to build a friendship.

Although I repeatedly use the term *friendship*, I am not in any sense intending the connotations of so-called friendship evangelism, which I believe to be a mistaken method of bringing people into the kingdom using relationship as collateral to motivate conversion.

I'm talking about a *real* friendship.

Unlike the Western world, where you can go to a church for fifteen years and still only know two people—where your individual credentials make you a desirable or undesirable person—the Eastern world has had a far longer stretch of time to think about the nature of relationships: family and friends.

In the Middle East, the prevailing tribal system has endured for thousands of years. By far the most important credential one can possess is lineage. In other words, your last name says more than your résumé. The family values of Arab cultures are common across Islam, and these values come with consequences. Honor and courage are among the chief virtues of any Arab. Conversely, shame is an issue that cuts deep into the heart, and even the historical failures of the Arab people bring a sharp stab of pain if flippantly addressed. Having said this, a recent influx of Western perspective and corporate-style business has, in some ways, stirred the pot.

As mentioned before, when Muslims move to the U.S. or elsewhere in the West, they tend to stay within their tribal or family systems and often live near each other. However, as you might expect, this depends on a variety of factors. Every once in a while we'll meet a Muslim family in the U.S. that seems disconnected from their society. Perhaps a lucrative job lured them to a certain place, or they're isolated because of bad family relations. Still, chances are high that when you find one Saudi, you'll find twenty. Meet one Pakistani, and you'll discover they live on a block full of friends and family.

The key point is, don't be intimidated by the close-knit Muslim community. Jump right in. Introduce yourself and befriend the whole lot. They'll love you all the more for being brave enough to do that.

TALKING ABOUT GOD

In the Islamic personification of God, he is vast and unknowable. His wrath—not his love—is emphasized, although he is, in the Qur'an, attributed with mercy and forgiveness.

God's completeness and unity within himself renders him so untouchable and even aloof that the very idea of God coming to earth in human form is unthinkable. I know it is difficult to read this, and even more difficult to find it palatable enough to put into practice, but if you intend to carry on conversations with a Muslim, you should know that the term "Son of God" is rejected by Muslims because of a misunderstanding (and you would reject it too if you mistakenly thought God had a son through a sexual relationship with Mary). I'm not suggesting that you *deny* what you know to be true about God, but rather that you be sensitive to the differences in the two faiths, particularly at the beginning of a friendship. (For more about this, see the section in chapter five, "How Can God Have a Son?")

Actually, at this point, I like to take a different route than most Christians. The popular method is to try to explain the Christian beliefs and to argue the veracity and superiority of our faith. E. Stanley Jones, in *The Christ of the Indian Road*, describes this method as one that demolishes the beliefs of the other and then attempts to build a structure on the smoldering wreckage.

Don't do this. I recommend that you *don't* try to argue that Jesus actually is the Son of God. Don't deny it either, but remember that God will reveal himself to each individual in a unique way; we are only participants in God's grand plan for this person. Arguing the deity or sonship of Jesus will only reinforce preexisting barriers until the time is right. God may be saving some information for later, allowing each person to digest the truth one piece at a time.

I believe that the most important question of all is found in the annals of the New Testament and was aimed at Peter. Jesus asked, "Who do you say that I am?" (Matthew 16:15–16).

I believe that if we can introduce people to Jesus, he will take the responsibility of asking each person the same question. Jesus revealed himself to every person who earnestly sought him. Should we believe now that he has ceased to do so?

With that in mind, once again, I make it my responsibility only to point people to Jesus, allowing him to reveal himself through his teachings, his miracles, and his Spirit.

If you earnestly wish to open some communication with your Muslim friends, you are going to have to be sacrificial about it. Some of the most important words and phrases in your faith are going to have to be put on the shelf for a while. As Paul did, you have to be willing to be all things to all people, even to become "as those who are under a law," in order that you might gain some. To the earnest Muslim, however, this cannot be a mere act on your part. In my experience, everybody has a "fake-o-meter" and can tell when you're putting on an act for them.

Throughout my time in the Middle East, whenever we would host interns or different youth teams at our facility, I always had one rule: Be honest, be real.

Confess *your* faults. Treat others with *more* honor. Respect your friends' religion. Always assume that the person you are speaking with has a more holy life than you do, and treat them accordingly. Be the low man on the totem pole. Be the servant.

I was always surprised at the fruit that grew out of this approach. Once our Muslim friends realized we were actually interested in them, and that we were genuine, they were much more willing to pray together and study the life of Jesus.

I assume that some people will read this and believe that my approach is blasphemous. However, please take these thoughts of mine and pray about them. If you disagree with anything I say, compare it side-by-side with the teachings of Jesus, and always go with what you're getting from him.

CHAPTER 4

Women and Islam: Protecting the Purity of Women

One of the most common questions I hear is, "What's Islam like for women?"

Although everyone shares the same concern, some ask the question not only out of concern for the women but also out of criticism of Islam. This is understandable, to say the least.

One of Islam's glaring flaws *is* its medieval perspective on women's rights. But this problem is not universal, and I am happy to say that many Arab/Muslim nations have become aware of this deficiency and are moving to correct it.

Much depends on the country. Some are more liberal, like Tunisia or Lebanon. Some are more fundamentalist: Saudi Arabia, Iran, and Sudan. Others are completely secular—for instance, Albania and many of the former Soviet Republics.

Within the community of Islamic nations, some structure their government and justice according to Sharia, Islamic law.

Sharia is derived not only from the teachings of the Qur'an but also from the Hadith, the official teachings of Muhammad himself. Sharia was constructed during a period in which Islam was on the rise and mobile, both politically and militarily. It not only details the regulations required of each Muslim for personal devotion but also the theological curricula for governance.

Nations that follow the blueprints of Sharia have a parochial perspective on women's rights. This is because the model for Islamic law is about twelve centuries old. Sadly, most Islamic law was not codified during Islam's golden era, when science, learning, and tolerance were values of the Islamic empire. Rather, the strongest elements of Islamic law came about during a time when women were not equal to men.

In Islamic states today, the legal valuation of a woman is approximately half that of a man. It's an actual judicial stipulation in court cases, for inheritance, and for compensation.

For example, a daughter receives half the entitlement a son does, and it takes the word of two women to counter the testimony of a man.

A woman is assumed to be of her husband's religion. If a Muslim man marries a Christian woman, she is a Muslim. Muslim men are permitted to marry Christian or Jewish women, but Muslim women cannot marry outside their faith.

In countries that are ruled by the Sharia, it is illegal to convert from Islam to another religion, the penalty sometimes resulting in death.

THE EVERYDAY LIVES OF MUSLIM WOMEN

There are some facts you should know about women in Islam, particularly if you plan on being a friend.

For the most part, the woman's place is the home. This is actually enforced in some countries. The Taliban, in particular, when it controlled Afghanistan, forced women out of their jobs, out of their schools, and back into their homes, which they could not leave without a male relative.

In most Muslim nations, women are not *required* to stay home—but it is often the reality. Throughout my years in the Middle East, I noticed how different groups of Muslims varied in their traditions. Most of our friends were the more liberal or even nominal variety, and the manners of the women were typically Western-leaning.

As mentioned before, honor is very important to Muslim

families, and it is within a woman's reach to bring dishonor on her whole family. As a result, women are "protected" from impurity and dishonor by staying close to home and, when away from home, being constantly under the watchful eye of a male family member.

Muslim women in the West face most of the same issues—good and bad—as they would in their home countries. If they are from a very conservative family, they are much more likely to also be conservative in dress and action when living in the West. If they come from a more liberal (open-minded) family, it would be rare to see them wearing a head covering, and they could likely hold a high-paying professional job like any other woman. Again, it all depends on the family, their version of Islam, and the social mores they live by.

In general, sexuality is suppressed among Muslim females, whereas flirting and even promiscuity tend to be more accepted behaviors for males, depending on their individual devotion to Islam.

Sadly, in the darker corners of Islamic culture, there still exists a propensity to punish women for sexual crimes perpetrated against them. For example, if a woman is raped, her male relatives might physically abuse her or even perform an "honor killing," murdering her to "protect" the family from dishonor. Although I personally don't know a single Muslim man who would even imagine committing such an atrocity, it must be noted for the sake of honesty.

This may also give you a direction in which to focus your efforts and your prayer.

The Qur'an is explicit about how women should dress:

> And say to the believing women that they should lower their looks and guard their modesty; that they should not display their beauty and ornaments except what (ordinarily) appear thereof; that they should draw their veils over their bosoms and not display their beauty except to their husbands, their fathers, their husbands' fathers, their sons, their husbands' sons, their brothers or their brothers' sons, or their sisters' sons, or their women, or the slaves whom their right hands possess, or male attendants free of sexual desires, or small children who have no carnal knowledge of women. (Q 24:31)

Interestingly, the ayat/verse prior to this one discusses the purity of *men*:

> Say to the believing men that they should lower their gaze and guard their modesty: that will make for greater purity for them: and Allah is well acquainted with all that they do.

The head-covering and accompanying veil that some Muslim women wear are known as *abaya,* or *hijab.* In conservative Islamic states like Saudi Arabia they are required. Punishment for disobedience of the law is severe and is usually carried out by a male relative in a display of devotion to Islam and to reclaim honor lost by the offender. In other Islamic states, the abaya is traditional, although not legally required. In the West it is an item of controversy, and if you befriend a Muslim woman in your city, you would be wise to make her feel comfortable with whatever decision she makes regarding traditions.

The typical homebound status of Muslim women—as well as their disposition as secondary to men—can make them hungry for friendship. Because Muslims honor purity, it is best if men befriend men and women befriend women, particularly when meeting in a home or alone. Even the slightest suggestion of immorality can ruin your relationship.

Muslim men and women often fear Western influence and corruption: Keep this in mind if you intend to help "modernize" the beliefs of your Muslim friend.

Remember too that the goal is to bring Jesus into your relationship—*not* Westernism, materialism, postmodernism, feminism, capitalism, or any other -ism.

The Saudi Princess

A few years ago my friend Frank (not his real name) and I arranged to meet a Saudi princess through a mutual friend. There are possibly three thousand Saudis in the royal family, connected by direct lineage or marriage to the house of Saud. These princes and princesses are generally affluent members of society, and many of them are well traveled and have some of the finest education available to them.

We met the princess at her home. She entertained us with traditional tea, and we sat down to talk. There were about six people present and, as usual, the conversation soon turned into the snake pit: politics. I *hate* talking about politics—somebody always gets hurt.

The princess had a unique perspective, however. She was a well-educated, highly intelligent member of the royal class, with a degree in journalism, of all things. Some of her work had been published in national presses, and she used her intellect and position to discuss women's rights, cultural instability, and the conflict between Westernism and entrenched Islamic traditions. Throughout, she remained respectful of Islam, as it was the religion of her people; at the same time, she clearly had a deep sense of offense toward the West—America in particular.

As she became more vocal and adamant, delivering one criticism after another in perfect English, we could tell it was *personal* to her—not merely a political argument. It had become a monologue until Frank spoke up. "Look, one thing's really obvious about all of this."

Perhaps anticipating some retaliation, she snapped, "What is that?"

"Well," he said, leaning forward with his elbows on his knees, "you've been hurt very badly, and I'm sorry for that. I really am."

"Excuse me?" she said, taken back. "What do you mean?"

"I can tell you're very intelligent, and you're very knowledgeable about East-West conflicts. But I can tell your feelings on these issues don't come from your education or your work. They come from your heart . . . and your heart, Princess, is wounded."

I looked over at Frank and saw a glint of moisture in his eyes. I couldn't believe it. We were in the middle of a heated discussion and Frank was starting to cry. He was doing what Jesus does—looking at the heart with compassion—while I had been getting angry.

The princess broke.

After a few minutes she looked up and wiped her eyes. "You are right. I am hurt, and I see no way out of it. I'm trapped in the layers of politics and religion and culture." She paused. "I have spent all of my life to find some meaning, something to belong to, and it always circulates back to the same old things again. It's so disappointing. I try to reach the people of Saudi Arabia to give them hope, and I have no hope myself."

"But let me ask you a question, if I may," I interjected. "What if I told you there was a kingdom much larger than Saudi Arabia, much greater than America, much deeper than the culture of Europe, and much richer than the religious institutions of Christianity or Islam. What would you say to that?"

The princess looked over her shoulder toward her uncle, who was standing nearby. We had to be wary— the slightest hint of irreverence would bring our conversation to an end. Her uncle nodded. He seemed to know that we meant no harm.

I continued. "Would you be interested in a kingdom of hope?"

"Certainly," she said. "Does God offer this hope?"

"Yes," I said, "and he has made a gateway to it—an entrance to this kingdom."

She looked suspicious for a moment. "Are you trying to tell me I should convert to Christianity?"

"No, we're not." I held up my hand for a moment. "Princess, what does the word *Muslim* mean to you?"

"Well . . . in the traditional sense, it means 'submitted.'"

"Yes, but what does it mean *to you*? What do you want it to mean?"

She shook her head. "I'm not sure what you're saying."

Frank picked up seamlessly where I left off. "Princess, what if 'submitted' could mean 'to belong to'? You spoke to us about hope, about significance, about meaning. If you can find these things with Allah, in this kingdom, would you not be the truest form of Muslim? Would you not truly be submitted to God?"

"Do I have to change my beliefs?" she asked. "Because this is not tradition. God is aloof; he is unknown by men."

"But he *is* known by men," I replied, "and by women. He has made this kingdom available."

"He has? Is it paradise? Our reward in death?"

"Princess, it is here, now."

Before responding, she again looked over her shoulder to her uncle, who nodded approvingly.

"How can I have this kingdom?"

"Allah sent a prophet. The Qur'an tells us he is the *word of God*, that he is a spirit from God and sits close to God. His name is Isa, and he is near to God now."

She nodded. "You call him Jesus of Nazareth, the Messiah."

"Yes," I said. "We have spent our lives following him, belonging to his kingdom."

"How do you belong to his kingdom?"

"The first thing Isa preached was that the kingdom of heaven is at hand. I believe that to be truly submitted to Allah is to be with him in spirit, in his kingdom, and I believe that Isa can open that door for you because he is near to Allah."

She glanced once more at her uncle, then asked, "Can we pray to Allah and ask him to speak to us about his kingdom?"

And we did. Frank and I took turns asking God to reveal his kingdom to our new friend. As we prayed, the Spirit of God entered the room. Within moments we were all in tears. She then prayed for God's kingdom to enter into her heart through the anointed one—Jesus.

A CHRISTLIKE PERSPECTIVE

As you read that faith story, a few red flags probably were raised. That's okay.

The definitions and labels aren't all that important. The heart is. Jesus has different names in every culture. The word *God* is different in almost every language. Some Western Christians of the past have been overly focused on changing the culture and words to match what was perceived to be the "correct way" in their home culture, rather than allowing the Holy Spirit to lead the new believers down the path most appropriate (and faithful) to their context.

A friend of mine illustrated this point to me, asking, "What if I told you that Jesus was the pig of God?"

My jaw dropped. "I'd be a little offended. That's contrary to Scripture."

"Of course, but try telling that to a primitive tribe in [a non-Muslim part of] Indonesia."

"What do you mean?" I asked.

"It's an illustration I had to use once," he said. "They don't have sheep in Indonesia, so I had no way to explain the sacrifice of Jesus for their sins, other than to use a wild pig as an example instead."

It hit me then: *It was the reality of the sacrifice*, not the textbook verbiage, that mattered.

Laughing, he asked, "Do you think we'd have to import sheep into every people group on the planet before we tell them the Good News about Jesus?"

He was right. And in the same way, we don't have to import *our* culture and religious traditions and labels to tell people about Jesus. Jesus is compatible with every culture because he *is* the gospel, and he gives himself freely. Jesus looks for a change of heart; men look for a change of culture.

It's always a matter of the heart, and hearts changed by God lead to changed cultures.

So it is with the women of Islam. They are expected to practice the teachings of the faith, although they are considered Muslim by marriage anyway. But whether or not they practice outwardly, we have found that women are open and interested in the deeper things of faith.

A way to build rapport with a Muslim woman is to talk about *her* life, her heart, her experiences, and her beliefs. If we're truly living the model exemplified by Jesus Christ, we should make every attempt to make our assertions, questions, and compassion about the other person, not about us, not about life in America or Europe. Be real, but don't let the conversation turn into "how the West is better for women," because that isn't the point.

The point is that Jesus loves women as much as he does men. Use his stories to point this out: Mary Magdalene, the Samaritan woman, the woman caught in adultery, the woman with the perfume vial, and Mary sitting at Jesus' feet while Martha prepared the meal. Jesus himself said, "Only one thing is needed. Mary has chosen what is better, and it will not be taken away from her" (Luke 10:42). Just as Mary enjoyed Jesus' company, surely there are many Muslim women who long to enjoy the company of Jesus and his friends.

"I'm So Sorry"

This story comes from my wife, Chris.

One evening, Carl and I and some close friends took the light-rail train to downtown Denver. Soon we were strolling down the busy cobblestone streets, chatting and laughing on the way to our favorite restaurant.

While our hearts were united in conversation about our lives and the new challenges we were facing, I noticed a sweet-looking Muslim woman, modestly dressed and wearing a hijab. My heart immediately raced with excitement and my feet seemed to carry me without effort away from my husband and friends and to this lone traveler.

I stepped up beside her and smiled. "Hi, how are you?"

"Fine," she replied.

"Are you Jordanian, by any chance?"

"No, I'm Iraqi," she said with a bit of surprise in her voice.

"Welcome to America," I responded, not really knowing if she needed welcoming or not. I'm not sure why, but my heart was moved with compassion for her, and I added, "I'm so sorry for all the turmoil your country has experienced over the years."

To my surprise, she immediately said, "And I'm so sorry for your soldiers who have to suffer in my country."

Wow, when was the last time I'd heard something

like that? We both agreed that we longed for peace and that God was the answer. My new friend's eyes twinkled with a warmth that I've rarely seen. It seems a soft answer and a gentle spirit really does unleash a flood-gate of hearts poured out.

I rejoined our group after a few more minutes of conversation with this dear woman, and I thought, *Why don't I always initiate conversation in this way with strangers?* I pray the next person to meet this lady will take one more step forward in the long and often unknown chain of sharing Christ's love!

CHAPTER 5

Common Questions: A Knowledgeable Response

I've compiled the top five questions my Muslim friends ask me. Some want my opinions about Islam, others want to know more about Christian beliefs. My point is *not* to provide so-called talking points for theological rebuttal, but rather to give more insight into questions you will often encounter with Muslims who are eager to talk about God, Jesus, and the holy books.

1. "DO YOU BELIEVE THE QUR'AN IS GOD'S INSPIRED BOOK?"

This is a common question—Muslims want to know what we think of their holy book—but it might surprise you to find that many Muslims have never read the Qur'an. They are aware of the structure of Islam from tradition rather than close study.

I always encourage Muslim friends to read the Qur'an. When they do, it usually leads to a series of questions, and because the Qur'an encourages Muslims to read the Gospels, I often see fruit from this endeavor. However, if a Muslim friend directly asks, "Is the Qur'an a holy book from God?" you have a theologically heavy issue to deal with. Don't take it lightly; this is extremely important to a Muslim.

First, realize that the Qur'an would never have been written unless God allowed it to be written. Although some might see this approach as a dodge, I would challenge them to think deeper: Look at the Qur'an as a book that can propel people to become curious about Jesus. I stress this always, because Jesus *is* the way, and any method or way to come to him is legitimate if the seeker actually finds Christ as the answer to the soul's burning need. Even Jesus, when his disciples objected to a believer outside their small group casting out demons and healing people in his name, approved the activity (Mark 9:38–40), because there is *no other name by which people can be saved* (Acts 4:12).

Another way to view this issue is to actually examine the

veracity of the Qur'an, which means reading it for yourself. While this can be time-consuming, it will give you rewards in terms of your friendships because you will have gained credibility to talk effectively about the Qur'an. And there's no way you can make decisions regarding truth in its contents without being knowledgeable enough to do so anyway. At the very least, you will have read a book highly revered by a fifth of the earth's population!

The final option is to simply deny any supernatural credence to the Qur'an right up front, which I don't recommend. There are no long-term benefits in doing so, and "winning" that point may cost in the long run. Again, the rule of thumb: Be sensitive. Remember that the concept of holiness is different to a Muslim, and this perspective is at least deserving of respect.

2. "DO YOU BELIEVE MUHAMMAD IS A TRUE PROPHET OF GOD?"

Again, think this question through before making a knee-jerk reaction. Ask yourself, "What is a prophet, anyway?" I believe it's important to verify *every* self-claimed prophet, whether they're in your church or in a mosque.

Here's my advice: Recognize that Muhammad wanted his people to return to the one true God, and demonstrate your respect for that tradition. But don't get caught in a debate about Muhammad. Always move back toward common ground: Jesus. Base your position on the things Muhammad said about Jesus instead of making an opposition based on the differences. Later on, I know it is logical to wonder where and how the teachings differ, and to want to try to argue them, but I believe there are many customs, traditions, and practices we can respect *while* we begin to explain the Good News of Jesus.

3. "HAS THE BIBLE BEEN CHANGED?"

As mentioned before, this is a common belief among Muslims. Many are taught that God revealed himself to the Israelites and later to the Christians, and yet the "people of the book" changed and distorted the teachings of God, such that the Bible can be misleading.

There are ways to handle this. Rather than defense, I think it is better to bring all of the relevant material back to Jesus and keep the discussion there, because Jesus reveals truth.

If, however, you feel it is the right time in your relationship to begin pushing the boundaries, you can point out what the Qur'an itself says about the Bible. Interestingly, several verses in the Qur'an seem to indicate the opposite of the claims that the Bible has "been changed."

- The Taureh was given to Moses by God: *"We [God] gave Moses the Book and followed him up with a succession of Messengers"* (Q 2:87); *"We did indeed aforetime give the book to Moses: so be not then in doubt*

of its reaching (thee): and We made it a guide to the
Children of Israel" (Q 32:23).

- The Zabur was given to David by God: ". . . And to
  David we gave the Psalms" (Q 4:163).

- The Injeel was given to Jesus the Messiah by God:
  "We sent after them Jesus the son of Mary, and
  bestowed on him the Gospel" (Q 57:27).

- Numerous times the Qur'an says of itself that it is
  a confirmation of the book (the Bible) that "was
  before it," including: "And this is a Book [the Qur'an]
  which we have sent down, bringing blessings, and
  confirming (the revelations) which came before it [the
  Bible]" (Q 6:92).

A STORY OF FAITH

Praying With a Hezballah Leader

Right there in the middle of a Lebanese Parliament building. Second floor. Office down the hall on
the right. I sat stunned, realizing tears were streaming
down the face of the leader of the twenty-five-member
Hezballah bloc. I had just prayed for him—a "regular
prayer," for blessing, health, wisdom, more revelation
of Jesus Christ in his life. But I didn't expect the burly,
bearded man would cry!

A month earlier I had met Ahmad at our prayer gathering in the Parliament. He was one of ten leaders with

whom we talked about prayer, faith, and Jesus. As we gathered in a circle to hold hands and pray at the end of the two-hour meeting, Ahmad was visibly touched.

I returned to visit him as soon as I could. His position in the country is quite influential as the Hezballah have grown in stature. Many in the West consider them a terrorist organization, but to the Shi'ites of Lebanon (nearly 40 percent of the country), they're heroes. They run schools, hospitals, and all types of humanitarian aid. They also have a military wing used to resist Israel.

He was so touched by what I shared that day, and by my prayer at the end, that he begged me to stay so he could introduce me to others in the Parliament. Unfortunately, I couldn't because we were scheduled to fly out the next day. He made me promise to get in touch as soon as I returned—a promise I was eager to keep!

About a month later we met again. We talked again about personal life, faith, and world issues. As I got up to say good-bye, he said, "Wait, aren't you going to do that thing again that you did last time you were here?"

"What thing?"

He didn't know what to call it, but he rubbed his thumb and finger together and said, "It gave me a good feeling."

"Oh, you mean when I prayed for you. I'd love to do that 'thing' again."

Muslims do pray. However, they don't always associate our informal style of prayer with what they call prayer. Although there is a version of informal prayer for Muslims, they would typically think of praying as the more ritualized, several-times-a-day version. So when I had prayed the time before, it was so spontaneous and natural that it didn't occur to him that it was a "prayer."

But pray I did. I prayed for his family, his heart, his country. And he cried. The burly, bearded leader of the Parliament for the Hezballah cried. When he regained his composure, he asked me to come and "do this thing to the other members of his party." Of course, I was happy to do that very "thing" with them and many others.

Prayer is a key factor in relating to our Muslim friends in a spiritual fashion. Unfortunately, Muslims often think that Christians don't believe in prayer because they don't see us praying formally the way they do. It's the same with fasting. Because we don't fast with them during the month of Ramadan, they assume we don't fast at all. While we don't want to make a public display out of our faith by praying or fasting just to be seen (Jesus tells us not to do this), we can let our Muslim friends know that we do pray by praying with and for them—out loud, while together.

Praying with and for our friends is powerful on several levels. It creates a unique bond with someone when you pray for them. It encourages them that you'd take the time to stop and pray. It shows them that you care enough to ask, "How can I pray for you?" And it allows God to work where you and I won't be able to.

Prayer is powerful. I try to pray with people that I

meet whenever I can. Muslims are particularly open to this. Try it!

---

4. "HOW CAN GOD HAVE A SON?"

To the Muslim, the idea of Jesus being transferred to earth as a "word from God" or a "spirit from heaven" is normal—that's what the Qur'an teaches. And, as mentioned before, the Qur'an *does* refer to "Isa the Messiah" and "Isa the Christ." So the question is not whether Muslims believe in Jesus. No, the *cornerstone* difficulty we face is that Muslims do not believe Jesus is the Son of God.

In fact, in Islam it is a serious transgression to make any person equivalent with God, and the concept of the Trinity (which, again, many Muslims think is God, Mary, and Jesus) is sacrilegious. Moreover, when we call Jesus the "Son of God," many Muslims think it means God had relations with a human woman to produce an offspring: Jesus. They decry this as ludicrous and blasphemous. So do we!

Sometimes I've found it tempting to simply say, "Jesus is who he said he was," and then leave it at that. But that's not really fair; he always needs explanation. Of course, he himself is The Point, but how we present him and explain him does make a huge difference. The more we know him, the better we can do this.

It often works to explain that the Bible does not teach that God was a man who had a baby boy named Jesus.

5. "WAS JESUS CRUCIFIED?"

Muslims think it is against God's nature, or even his capability, to allow such a prophet to be killed by human hands. Instead, they believe God was "above" the execution of Jesus by tricking the Jews and the Romans into *believing* that he'd been crucified. At the same time, Muslims believe that Jesus ascended to God, and that at the end of time he will come to earth again.

It is interesting to note that more and more Muslim scholars acknowledge that there is room in the Qur'an for interpreting several passages as allowing for the death and resurrection of Jesus.

Let me tell a story to explain my thoughts about discussing Christ's death with Muslims. Several years ago in a home in downtown Beirut, I met with a group of Muslim businessmen and political leaders. We were having a vibrant discussion about Jesus in the gospel of Luke when a friend of the others walked in. When he realized what we were doing, he said, "But we're Muslims. How can you be talking about Jesus with *that man?*" He pointed at me. "He believes that Jesus was crucified, and we do not."

All heads turned to see my reaction. In years past I would have reverted to an apologetic approach, explaining to our new friend that indeed the Bible does teach that Jesus died and rose again, and that he should believe that too in order to obtain eternal life. But instead, my response surprised even me. I looked at him, smiled, and shrugged my shoulders, lifting my hands up as if to say, "What's your point?"

The awkward silence spurred the others to come to my rescue and turn on their friend. "Why did you have to bring *that* up? We were having a nice discussion about Jesus before you came in!" The visitor sat down with a sigh and we continued reading through Luke.

Now, you may be wondering if I think it's important for my Muslim friends to know and understand the death and resurrection of Jesus Christ. Of course! Vital. But we often forget that Jesus died at the *end* of his earthly life, not the beginning. We do present "Christ crucified" but not necessarily on day one. Let the story be one with a beginning, a middle, and an end.

I often like to say to my friends in the Muslim world, "Let's talk about Jesus. Let's discuss his life, his teachings, his ways." A complete study of the life of Jesus will bring the student to understand his death and resurrection in the right time and in the right way.

A CHRISTLIKE PERSPECTIVE

The first step in talking about matters of faith is one of immense self-control and a deep desire to present Jesus to your Muslim friend: Drop the arguments and forget the fight. It isn't about who's *more* right and who's *more* wrong. It's about pointing toward Isa (Jesus) and allowing his Spirit to do the heavy lifting.

Take the questions you receive seriously. They are not

mere discussions: They often involve the very articles of faith for your Muslim friend, who will do whatever it takes in an argument to uphold the sovereignty of God. Muslims do not accept anything that they perceive lessens God's greatness. God is unimpeachable in his greatness.

This gives you a tremendous opportunity. You can always be respectful with the questions and topics of discussion while simultaneously being genuine and enthusiastic about Jesus.

Ask questions yourself. But don't pry. You can gain the respect of your friend by showing that you are a seeker also. Engage your friend with questions that give you both something to think about.

CHAPTER 6

Jesus Meets Jihad: Overcoming Fear With Love

Not long ago I was talking to a new neighbor about my experiences in the Middle East. We had been working in our gardens, opposite each other, when we introduced ourselves.

I found out he was a deacon at his church. And when he asked what I did, I told him about my work and my friends in Lebanon. Admittedly, I gave him the best stories. After all, who wants to make a poor first impression?

"Wow," he said, leaning over the fence with his gardening

gloves on and a pair of clippers in one hand. "Although I admire what you've done with your life, I can say, without a doubt, I would never do anything like that."

"You never know unless you try," I said, half joking. "Seriously, though, what *would* you do about your convictions in light of the condition of the world?"

"You get right to the point, don't you?" He took a moment before continuing. "I'd like to say that I would *try* to reach out to Muslims, to tell them about Jesus, even to help them with their lives—you know, to be compassionate."

"Okay," I said, "but what would you *really* do? Pretend you're in a position to make the decision."

He blew a long breath out and rubbed his chin. "I think I would squash the whole region. Cut the losses, end the debate."

"Wow," I said, "thanks for your honesty. But tell me, how can you reconcile that with what you know Jesus would want you to do?"

"See, that's the catch. It makes no difference. I'm a blue-collar worker in Denver, and the only thing I know about Islam is what I see on CNN. So for all intents and purposes, it doesn't matter. I have my beliefs and my convictions, but I'm not in any position to do anything about them. I'm irrelevant."

I stayed up late that night, trying to read, and yet the conversation haunted me. *He can't really believe he's irrelevant,* I thought.

Then again, I had spent half my life in the middle of it all; he had not. My experiences had led me to believe that what I felt in my heart toward Jesus and my Muslim friends was always immediately relevant. I couldn't talk about Jesus with bitterness or prejudice toward these people. I couldn't even talk to *them* if I was double-minded about everything.

Most Western Christians are not guilty of this double-mindedness by choice. On one hand, they know what they read in the Gospels is true, but on the other hand, they live in a time of color-coded terror alerts and can't even take a domestic flight without wondering if it will be their last.

IS ISLAM SAFE TO REACH OUT TO?

What my neighbor said in two minutes describes a shadow that has fallen over many of us. Not only do people wonder if Islam is safe enough to reach out to, but they struggle to have the compassion of Christ to do so.

It's easy to believe the problem is Islam itself. No doubt religion is a hotbed for deep convictions, zealous emotions, and, at times, fiery conflicts. But there is nothing gained by accusing a religion of brokering violence committed by a handful of its followers.

Christine Mallouhi, author, speaker, and Christian member of a Muslim family, points out that "real Christians, Muslims, and Jews do not murder. Terrorists murder and terrorists do not discriminate for *a terrorist's religion is hate and terror*"[1] (emphasis added).

I agree. But too often I have heard one person or another, fed up with international terrorism, say something like, "It's time we quit making excuses for them and just call a spade a spade." They think murder and Islam are synonymous.

I typically respond with: "You're absolutely right. Murderers are murderers, and we should stop making excuses for them."

Many of my friends are military personnel, and a common phrase I hear from their collective input is: "The priority is to secure the region. Once we have removed threats and built a representative government, then we can continue with religion and social welfare."

One friend in particular, frustrated by my point of view, once blurted, "Look, Carl, we can't tell people about Jesus if they destroy themselves or kill us. Your altruistic perspective doesn't take the human factor into account. You can't share God's love with someone when you're dying under a mushroom cloud."

If we're answering the question "Is it safe to go to Muslim countries?" then I'd simply say it's as safe as it was to take the Gospel to the nations when Jesus first commanded it. However, it may be the wrong question, which then leads us to the wrong answer. Maybe it's not about safety

---

[1] Christine A. Mallouhi, *Waging Peace on Islam* (Downers Grove, IL: InterVarsity Press, 2002), 158.

or wondering if "they" might kill us, but what is the clear command of Christ: Go into *all* the world . . .

COUSINS IN CONFLICT

One thing needed is a wider understanding of the brutal history of conflict between what have been labeled the "three great monotheisms." The birth of Judaism is attributed to Abraham and Moses; Christianity adopts these two forefathers, plus it attempts to follow the revolutionary life, death, and resurrection of Jesus Christ. Hundreds of years later, Islam emerges and claims the same lineage: Abraham, Moses, and Jesus.

The widespread Christian perspective for some time has been that because Islam was founded after Judaism and Christianity, it is not a genuine monotheistic faith, and its Arabian roots are not really of Abraham at all. Often we disregard Islam offhandedly as a fake, all the while injuring Muslims and mocking the sincerity of their faith. Judaism, however, is seen more favorably because it is part and parcel of the faith in the same one true God.

I am not suggesting that all three monotheistic faiths are the same, but I do want to point out that every Muslim believes his religion is also directly connected to Abraham. So why argue this point? Faith in Abraham is not the issue.

The earliest division within Islam itself happened literally the day after Muhammad died in 632. According to Karen Armstrong, Abu Bakr, the first *caliph* (leader) "was chiefly preoccupied by the so-called wars of *riddah* (apostasy)when various tribes tried to break away from the *ummah* and reassert their former independence."[2] The well-known division between Sunni and Shi'a Islam separated those Muslims who believed that the keepers of the teaching of Muhammad (the *Sunna*, or teachings) should lead the movement and those who followed a relative of Muhammad, a son-in-law named Ali.

The party of Ali (*Shi'a Ali*) became known as the Shi'a, or Shi'ite, sect, and today they comprise only about 15 percent of the Muslim world, primarily in Iran. There is also a growing presence of Shi'a Islam in Iraq.

The primary difference between Sunni (see below) and Shi'a is that the Shi'ites believe Ali was the first rightful caliph. Today, the word *imam* is used.

These imams are directly descended from Ali himself; they are considered righteous, and, to some, even infallible. They do not recognize any imam who is outside the bloodline of Ali, and they commemorate the martyrdom of Hussein with quite a festival.

Sunni Muslims constitute the majority of mainstream Islam, from the more nominal Muslim population to some of the most repressive dictatorships in the world. They do not believe the imamate line of Shi'a Ali is the solely legitimate source of Muslim leadership. Also, in countries where Sharia is enforced, it is considered to be immutable, and

---

[2] Karen Armstrong, *Islam: A Short History,* Modern Library ed., Modern Library Chronicles (New York: Modern Library, 2000), 25.

to change it would be to break it—bringing strict consequences.

Sunni Islam typically oppresses its minority Shi'a cousins through persecution, political superiority, and in some cases, outright bloodshed, notably in Iraq during Saddam Hussein's reign.

From 1979 on, under Saddam Hussein, the ruling Baath party (a secular political party comprised mostly of Sunnis) killed the Shi'ites of southern Iraq with the same ferocity they used on the Kurdish people of the north.

Despite this violence, the vast majority of Muslims are like you and me: They want to have a safe and peaceful life with their family and friends. It's an extremely small percentage of Muslims who think that some sort of violence is allowable or encouraged by the Qur'an. My experience has consistently been that the vast majority of Muslims condemn all forms of violence done "in the name of Islam." It's spoken of widely on TV and in print that the ones who are most hurt by terrorism are Muslims themselves. Unfortunately, we don't get to see that in the Western media.

Today, the extreme faction of Islam includes groups such as the Taliban of Afghanistan, the Muslim Brotherhood, and the Wahhabi sect of Saudi Arabia.

THE ORIGINS OF JIHAD

The roots of anger are deep and tangled amidst the shared history of Judaism, Christianity, and Islam. At various times, wars, politics, and zeal for both God and real estate have brought these three into conflict. Campaigns have been launched against each other and variously called "holy war" or "jihad."

The following information—none of which I mean to be "the final word"—is from my college days when I was slaving away for my degree, and also from firsthand conversations with primary sources (i.e., Muslims). I think it is important because it can shed some insights into the hearts and minds of even everyday Muslims.

Muslims are wounded people, injured by the stigma attached to them because of radical movements. It may seem unreasonable, but I've noticed that some Muslims actually have the same fear of us that we have of them. Because of the many centuries of division and fighting between the Big Three monotheisms, potential hot buttons and land mines are plentiful in any relationship. So make an earnest decision not to be defensive, retaliatory, or presumptuous. It is about you, your friend, and Jesus, not about religious institutions or the history of hatred and shame.

For Muslims, a low point in their history came when the Turkish Ottoman empire finally crumbled at the end of World War I under the weight of European military forces. This sounded a death knell of sorts for much of the once-proud Islamic empire. Centuries before, Islam had extended as far north as middle France and as far south as sub-Saharan Africa, and stretched from Gibraltar in the west to Kashmir in the east. The vast and militant empire was ruled by a collection of caliphs—social, spiritual, political, and military leaders of their people.

When the Ottoman Turks finally surrendered to Western military forces, the empire relinquished control to Catholic/Protestant Christians, and the rope of Islamic unity unraveled into warring nations, tribes, and colonies newly owned by various European monarchies.

Controlling, conniving, and often corrupt, these colonial usurpers maligned the character of Jesus. They often did the opposite of what he had preached: "If anyone asks for your tunic, give him your shirt also." The colonial powers did not give—they exploited. While traditional Islam described Jesus as a sinless prophet, Muslims saw sinful profit. At *their* expense.

From Anger to Forgiveness

As Chris and I walked into the lobby of the five-star hotel, already buzzing with afternoon activity, my heart was in my throat. It was 4:20, and people were everywhere, even though the Iftar meal (which breaks each day's fast during Ramadan) wouldn't start for another twenty minutes.

We greeted the host and hostess (our doctor friends) and then had our pictures taken by a local paper. (Yuck.) For several weeks, I had felt full of faith about speaking at this Doctors' Association event, but now I felt sick. I couldn't even eat the food (at first).

Making the night more dramatic was news that the Israeli army had gone into Bethlehem earlier that day and destroyed several houses and shot and killed a young boy who was a bystander. The region was in an uproar. In fact, the event was almost canceled, and my doctor friend considered asking me not to speak.

With about seven hundred people in attendance, I hadn't felt so scared since junior high. But as soon as I opened my mouth, I sensed the presence of God. I spoke for about fifteen minutes without translation. (Mahmoud then read the speech in Arabic, so they heard it twice.)

I had titled the talk, "From Retaliation to Reconciliation," and I made sure to address a few specific things. First, I felt the Lord leading me to be honest and open— not to just give a speech. Second, I knew I needed to connect with these people at the heart level. Third, I knew I needed to share with them our need for love, repentance, and forgiveness. A tall task indeed. All in a few minutes.

I began by stating that I knew the reason for all the world's problems and how to solve them. That seemed to get everyone's attention. Then I shared how we each need to repent of the sin in our hearts and not worry what others are doing. I retold Jesus' "log in the eye" story and announced that I was the problem. The issue in the world was me. I was the Big Sinner in the story, and all the wars in the world were reflected in my own heart.

I told them my own heart harbored fear. Anger. Frustration. And I told them I needed their help and their forgiveness. But mostly we needed the forgiveness of God, I said. We needed to go beyond "understanding" and "dialogue" and get down to a personal heart-to-heart level.

I quoted Luke 6:37: "Do not judge, and you will not be judged. Do not condemn, and you will not be condemned. Forgive, and you will be forgiven."

I begged them to respond when I again asked for their forgiveness. Many actually called out, "We forgive you, Carl." My talk ended with a standing ovation and a long line of people thanking me afterward.

Later, Mahmoud called me and described the night as historic. He thought it was the first time that a non-Muslim, non-politician American had spoken at a Ramadan Iftar in Lebanon. And it was definitely the first time he had heard an American or a Christian ask Muslim Arabs for forgiveness.

After the speech, I was also encouraged by what a general in charge of the Ministry of Interior had said: "Thank you for being so honest. What you spoke about is what we need in Lebanon. I want to make sure this message gets into all the newspapers, and I'd like to be in touch."

Once again, the power of the simple message of love, forgiveness, and peace showed that it conquers all. It's the way of Jesus. The world is full of strife, war, conflicts, and hatred. The life Christ offers is the opposite of that: He provides a way to live in this very world, but to do so in peace and love. But we have to choose this stand. It doesn't come easily or naturally.

CONFLICTING VIEWPOINTS

There is so much fear of the unknown Islamic faith that all Muslims are often blamed for the violence of a few. Still, it is important to acknowledge that Western policies sometimes create tensions and add insult to injury regarding the Muslim sense of honor, which runs very deep.

In 1953, the CIA backed an operation to overthrow the Iranian president and place the Shah of Iran in power. The West saw this as a rational act to create a balance of power and to offset Soviet aggression in the region, but Shi'ites in Iran had a completely different viewpoint. An intrusion of unwelcome Western influence into the only remaining Shi'a Islamic nation was neither stabilizing nor protective; it was exploitation.

In 1979, American "stabilization" efforts were shattered when supporters of Ayatollah Khomeini overthrew the Shah and stormed the U.S. Embassy. In the U.S., this was viewed as outright hostility. To the Iranian Shi'ites, it was a reassertion of the natural order. They had recovered their nation, rejected Western influence, and had a leader who could once again unite them.

During the early 1980s, the United States sponsored—with Saudi and Pakistani help—the arming, training, and funding of the *mujahedin,* the freedom fighters of Afghanistan. They were a ready-and-willing buffer of Islam against the advances of Soviet expansion. With American weapons and money these Afghans contained the Soviet forces within the major cities.

This caused a change of perspective within Islam. Instead of Islamic nations being at the mercy of Western influence, this time the West had relied on them. America needed the mujahedin in order to check Soviet expansion. Within the Muslim community, pride rose, with a need for recognition. A debt had accrued, but where was the payment?

Instead, America forgot about the Afghan and Tajik Muslims who had vanquished the iron curtain. The Soviet empire fell and, with it, American reliance upon these cunning fighters dissipated.

At this point, we need to consider: Where was al-Qaeda primarily based? Afghanistan. Where was al-Qaeda's financial support? Saudi Arabia. Where did al-Qaeda go to build their intelligence resources? Pakistan.

A band of Muslim brothers arose, eager for leadership, forgotten by former friends, and without a place to call their own. And thus (it is speculated), the Taliban was born. (*Talib* means *student.*)

Again we fast-forward. After years of subliminal communication between post-Soviet-threat America and Iraq, a ruthless dictator named Saddam Hussein decided that because the real estate of Kuwait was a historical province of Iraq, he should take it back for the expansion of the nation—and to add more oil fields. The American response was Operation Desert Shield, with military forces deployed to the region for the sake of Kuwait, a key U.S. ally.

From the Western standpoint, this looked like a completely appropriate action. Kuwait was an ally—mostly defenseless—and Saddam Hussein was a wicked despot who didn't bat an eye at the thought of killing thousands. An easy choice.

But the consequences, although not immediate, were severe. Saudi Arabia needed U.S. intervention in order to ensure that Hussein's Iraqi army would not flood further south into the peninsula. Saudi Arabia gave the United States a strategic landing point from which to deploy forces: its own territory. To the West, this seemed logical, reasonable, and perhaps even arbitrary.

To Islam it looked like this: Western Christian forces were being given access to the holiest of all lands. Saudi Arabia is the home of Mecca and Medina, the two most sacred cities in Islam. From this vantage point, the *infidels* (nonbelievers) were given access to attack Iraq, a secular-led nation of Muslims. To the earnest Muslim, this was sacrilege, the allegiance of the U.S. to Kuwait notwithstanding. Meanwhile, Saudi finance continued to flow (with or without government knowledge) into the growing Taliban movement in Afghanistan and even into Pakistan.

Of course, the longest lasting tensions in the Middle East have run through the heart of the Holy Land. I may be biased, but it seems that the West has pledged allegiance to the state of Israel at the expense of its Arab neighbors. Much of this is surely due to the Jews suffering so brutally during the Nazi years. Our compassion has encouraged us to stand behind the Jewish people as they regain their homeland. And many of those returning to Israel have been our very own neighbors. Finally, our shared historical and theological/biblical heritage provides a natural bridge with our Jewish friends.

Still, we have sometimes taken this too far. Does God love one people at the expense of others? Amazingly, I have heard comments from the pulpit proclaiming the virtues of the nation-state of Israel while at the same time encouraging the virtual extermination of Palestinian Arabs attempting to share the same land.

I know my perspective regarding the Middle-Eastern conflict may be viewed as ignorant or simplistic to some. I do not, in any way, believe the existence of an Israeli state is questionable. I do not hold a side when it comes to geo-political distinctions, and I do not believe that any person has the right to bomb, shoot, burn, or defile the people and/or presence of another culture in order to gain religious or political dominance. War is always a tragedy. Surely no one who bears the name of Christ would consider calling for the destruction of Muslims, since it would seem contrary to so much of what Jesus commanded.

A STORY OF FAITH

Bin Laden's "Cousins" Hear the Good News

The pitch-black night seemed to smother us as we walked down the narrow winding streets of Tripoli, Lebanon. I was accompanied by my Lebanese friend Hasher and my American friend John. We were going to meet with the top leadership of the Salafi Muslim sect. The Salafis are out of the same theological Islamic mold as the Taliban of Afghanistan. They are basically first cousins to al-Qaeda and the Taliban from the Wahhabi tradition in Saudi Arabia.

By the time we turned a corner and stepped through a small narrow door into a small, dark room—well, I was wondering what in the world I was doing. (Once again.)

Inside I was shocked by the sight of about fifty men who looked exactly like Osama bin Laden. All with long beards and robes, they spoke only the classical Arabic, not the colloquial Lebanese version I was used to. My heart was pounding! These men had taken a vow to live according to the most extreme version of Islam. Yet it seemed God had put us right in their midst that very night.

The meeting, which had been set up by Hasher, was to discuss the differences between Christianity and Islam. As you know by now, I'm not big on starting with our differences but rather prefer to begin with the things we share in common—mainly Jesus.

So within minutes our conversation turned to him.

We talked about Jesus Christ, his life, death, and resurrection, for nearly three hours. I finished by telling them that I loved them and that we know God loves them. They showered us with hugs, kisses, and well-wishes. It was another potentially scary situation that God turned into something powerful.

Their leader walked us out to the curb of the main street with these words: "You have broken down our stereotypes of what a Christian looks like and how they think. We so appreciate you taking the time to come here. I know it must have been hard. Would you please come back so we can talk some more about Isa al Masih? We love you and what you stand for."

Isn't it amazing that negative stereotypes go both ways! They have judged us as we have judged them. They are afraid of us like we are afraid of them. It's the love of Christ that breaks this barrier down so we can see and hear the Good News that's available to all.

A CHRISTLIKE PERSPECTIVE

This is the birthplace of my contention: Threats may loom, war may strike, and blood may be shed. But according to the Hebrew prophet Isaiah, "The word of our God stands forever" (40:8).

So where are we to stand, those of us who follow Jesus? I'm not talking about political distinctions. I'm referring to the conditions of our hearts. Many of us have differences:

things to mourn, thoughts to reconsider, beliefs to be reexamined.

I ask only this: Do not fall into the sea of those who believe they are irrelevant. For the spiritual person, there can be no apathy. We cannot allow copouts. After all, what is the distance between us and God? Often that distance can be covered by falling to our knees in genuine honesty. "Great are you, Lord; how great is your mercy." And, "My enemies mock me, my life is at stake," and "Forgive them, Father, for they do not know what they are doing."

There is deliverance and relief in the words of Jesus. There is forgiveness, compassion, and sometimes severity in his tone. It is true leadership—we would be stupid to ignore this. So why do we?

The condition of our hearts most determines whether we are relevant and significant or completely disconnected. No matter if you are not the president, a pastor, a soldier, a diplomat, or whatever—the condition of your heart is just as important, *for your sake*. By choosing an attitude of love and compassion toward people we don't understand, and toward an intimidatingly unknown religion, we not only see fear and suspicion diminish, we begin to build bridges. Bridges that lead to Jesus, the Prince of Peace.

Still, what are we to do about jihad? About the few Muslims who really *do* want to kill us?

It becomes very difficult to "love the sinner and hate the sin" when you believe you are the target. One of my friends once said, "That's like loving the bomb and hating the explosion." He has a point. But is this really a valid disclaimer, or is it a way to alleviate ourselves of the cross we are called to carry?

It goes without saying that if you want to reach a person, you have to look at him as an *individual*. The preconceptions you may have about Islam need to be discarded from the beginning if you want to have a genuine relationship with a Muslim. There can be no more generalizations and blanket distinctions.

To quote the late Mother Teresa of Calcutta:

> We all have the duty to serve God where we are called to do so. I feel called to serve individuals, to love each human being. *My calling is not to judge the institutions. I am not qualified to condemn anyone.* I never think in terms of a crowd, but of individual persons.
>
> If I thought in terms of crowds, I would never begin my work.
>
> I believe in the personal touch of one to one.
>
> If others are convinced that God wants them to change social structures, *that is a matter for them to take up with God*[3] (emphasis added).

Mother Teresa's exhortation to base the gospel from the "personal touch of one to one" echoes the wisdom and compassion of Jesus, who, while he was busy and surrounded by mobs, *continually* took the time to touch individual people with healing, forgiveness, admonition, and salvation.

[3] Mother Teresa, *In My Own Words* (New York: Gramercy Books, 1997), 99.

One-to-one relationships are key to fruitfulness, so forget evangelism as a methodology. You know how it feels when somebody approaches you with a religious angle. You don't like having evangelism "done" to you, so I don't advise "doing evangelism" to others.

Make it about building a true friendship, and let Christ change the heart. Simply present Jesus. Be interested, participate, ask questions, and above all, love and respect your friend. This is called discipleship (or mentoring). You don't start with a list of doctrines that need to be believed in order to convert; you start with simple friendship, one to one.

Again, always assume that your friend is more devoted than you, not less. I always tell my friends, "Boy, when I have my life as wholesome as yours, I'll have it made." They laugh, but it makes a point: I'm not assuming I'm better than them simply because I like talking about Jesus. If you act as if they are the sinner and you aren't, you won't be around them for very long.

Discipleship is the sum of time spent with somebody. Discipleship is not about the sinner's prayer or the end result. And discipleship is the root concept of Matthew 28:19, the Great Commission: "Go and make disciples of all nations. . . ."

CHAPTER 7

Standing on the Bridge: Muslims Who Follow Jesus

The most serious heresy for a Muslim is to leave Islam. Those who do are often abandoned, ostracized, cut off, and in some places, executed. To leave the path of God for anything is to invoke his wrath, and Muslims live in fear of this, which is where some of their devotion comes from.

As a result, I have come up with specific guidelines for talking to my Muslim friends about Jesus. The first thing I do is toss aside "the gospel of terminology." A case in point:

"I'm still a Muslim, though," a friend told me when I asked him if following Jesus meant he had become a Christian.

"Oh?" I said, curious.

"Yes," Ali said. "I am a Muslim who follows Jesus."

"How does *that* work?" I asked him. "What does your family think?"

He looked at me strangely and said, "They think nothing of it. I am a Muslim. What should they think?"

I had to ponder that for a minute, and then it hit me: Accepting Jesus as his teacher had taught Ali to make Jesus his leader, and in turn, had taken him to the revelation of who Jesus *really is*—Savior and Master. At no point had Jesus ever said to my friend, "You must change your name, go to a Western-style church, and give up your family and tribe."

Instead, Jesus said the same two words to Ali that he'd said to a couple of men in the same region about two thousand years ago: "Follow me."

HOPE

Truth be told, there is a growing number of Muslims around the world who maintain their cultural identity as "Muslim" but choose to align themselves with the spiritual and moral teachings of Jesus, becoming *his* disciples while becoming what "Muslim" truly means: submitted to God.

I know there is quite a bit of controversy over this issue. Some Christians may find it to be a disagreeable one, so we need to ask three key questions:

1. Is it *theologically* viable for a Muslim to refer to himself as a "follower of Jesus" and still be a Muslim?

2. Is it *culturally* feasible for a Muslim to remain a Muslim and follow Jesus?

3. Is there a need to become a "Christian" in *terminology* in order to follow Jesus in both theological and cultural fashion?

In all, we need to know if this concept lines up with the Scriptures and the teachings of Jesus himself, and if it will actually work in Muslim culture. Question #3 is the least important, but exploring whether or not the terminology of Christendom is important may be a bit of a pill for some people to swallow. It may be that Muslims in the Middle East can understand Jesus' parables more immediately than we; they certainly are closer to the culture of Jesus' day than are we. Furthermore, "Christian" in America looks a lot different from the way Peter understood it in first-century Palestine. Upon hearing the testimony of Cornelius, Peter was able to say that God accepted the Gentiles just as they were, by their faith in Jesus. When Peter's colleagues heard this, "they had no further objections and praised God, saying, 'So then, God has granted even the Gentiles repentance unto life'" (Acts 11:18).

In the context of history, a Muslim's identity is major. If he becomes a "Christian," the rejection will be immediate and final. If he can retain his cultural identity and yet follow Jesus without having to convert his religious *title* to Christianity, he benefits in that he can keep his family and his normal healthy relationships. He can also begin what I like to call "an insider movement toward Jesus as Christ."

There are some historical instances that seem to be exceptions to Muslims accepting Jesus as only a prophet, however great.

I was recently reading my friend Christine Mallouhi's book *Waging Peace on Islam*[1] (which I've quoted already in this book; it's a mainstay in my personal library), when I came across a chapter entitled, "The Mystical Influence in Islam." The following information is drawn from her work.

Christine wrote about the *Sufi* Muslims, originally monks who lived in seclusion from what they viewed as a widespread corruption of Islam. Many of them lived in intentional poverty, instead seeking nourishment spiritually, and many of them were completely dedicated to living according to the teachings of Jesus.

I was fascinated by this—fascinated by the way Jesus' wisdom and compassion had managed to find its way into the very heart of Islam.

The Sufis believed that to serve God was to love God, purely and simply. They rigorously expended themselves in songs and dances, in pure worship of this creator God who

---

[1] Christine A. Mallouhi, *Waging Peace on Islam* (Downers Grove, IL: InterVarsity Press, 2002).

made them so that they could live in a love relationship with him. They believed that all else was nothingness, a waste.

One eighth-century mystic, a woman named Rabia al-Adawiyya, said, "If I worship you [God] for fear of hell, burn me in hell." She firmly believed that God should not be loved out of fear but rather because he is worthy of her love and because he is beautiful. Christine wrote, "She longed to die in order to meet God."

(As a side note, the Sufis were one of the first religious sects to recognize the equality of men and women. Women could be Sufis and also teachers or leaders over men.)

Another Sufi, Ibn Arabi, who was loved by many and hated by more, is considered one of the greatest of all Muslim thinkers. He believed that Jesus was the word, the spirit, and the servant of God. Even God's mouthpiece. He once wrote, "The person who catches the disease of Christ can never be cured."

Yet another, Jalal al-Din Rumi, used his own interpretation of the ritual ablutions before prayer by saying, "Lord, wash me. My hand has washed this part of me, but my hand cannot wash my spirit. I can wash this skin, but you must wash me."

This flies directly against the typical Muslim concept of religion, in which the works of the flesh are critically significant. Rumi also believed that he could worship God in a Christian church, a Jewish synagogue, or a Muslim mosque because, as he put it, "I see one altar."

One Sufi was martyred for heresy because of such

convictions. He said, "On the supreme example of the Cross I intend to die. For I seek neither the Batha [Mecca] nor the Medina."

This mystic's name was Hussein Ibn Mansour Hallaj. He was tortured, burned, crucified, and dismembered for being a secret Christian in the eyes of his contemporaries. While he was tortured, he cried out, "By killing me you give me new life."

So the question is, would Jesus require a Muslim to "convert" to Christianity?

In actuality, Jesus never used the word *Christian*. For that matter, neither did Paul. Peter did once, telling others they might be insulted because of the name of Christ: "If you suffer as a Christian, do not be ashamed . . ." (1 Peter 4:14–16). *Christian* appears one other time in the Bible— in the book of Acts—where Luke says "the disciples were called Christians first at Antioch" (Acts 11:26). Even so, the origin of the word—"little Christs"—may have been used by non-Christians in Antioch in a derogatory way.

We are never commanded, exhorted, or encouraged to use the word *Christian*. It is, after all, a word, and for that matter a loaded word, weighted with hidden meanings and historical grievances. A much better phrase, one I use myself, is "follower of Jesus." This defines. It explains. It's dynamic and real. We really *are* following Jesus.

The reality is that Jesus was born a Jew and became a thorn in the side of the religious community, all the while developing a grassroots followership, for which he died in order to sacrifice himself for their sins.

It then follows that his personal mission was not to found a new religion called Christianity but rather to, as he said, "seek and save the lost." So, however we define this, we can agree that his identity, at least in his teaching and his lifestyle, was not "Christian."

Paul pushes it even further. He stated in Galatians 3:28 that "there is no longer Jew or Gentile . . . For you are all one in Christ Jesus" (NLT), showing us that obligatory cultural terminology does not carry any weight in the eyes of God. Those who are in Christ are in Christ; those who are not, simply aren't.

Being a Hope Broker

I met Mohsen one night at my friend's house. We were having a gathering of top-level Lebanese political leadership to discuss how these men could work with us in bridging the Arab East and American West. Mohsen was a Sunni Muslim parliament member and a striking man in every way. He was articulate, handsome, well dressed, and I later found out, spoke seven languages and sang Italian opera. He gave me a five-minute appointment at his office the next week.

When I arrived at the time scheduled, he was just leaving. He had forgotten our meeting. Embarrassed, he invited me to join him for lunch—at his house.

If you know anything about Arabs, you know their hospitality is famous. Typically, only the most basic small talk is engaged in until coffee and sweets are served. But in this case, after entering his house, he slouched down, put his head between his hands, and sighed. "Life's hard."

I asked him what was going on. He simply replied, "I have no hope. No hope for Lebanon whatsoever."

"That's pretty serious since you're a leader in the country. That's probably not good."

"Well, enough about me," he quickly said. "Tell me something about you. What do you do?"

"I'm a hope broker." (I had never said that before and have never used it since, but it seemed appropriate to the situation.)

"Hmm. What does a hope broker do exactly?"

Since I wasn't used to this line of questioning, I didn't really know what to say other than the obvious: "I deal hope."

"Well, where do you get it? The hope. Where do you get your hope?"

"First, tell me more about why things are so bad in Lebanon and what it's like to be in your position. Then I will tell you where I get hope." So he did. But within five minutes he remembered what I'd said and came back to it.

"So explain this 'hope thing' that you mentioned."

I began: "It's so simple it's almost silly. Here's the idea. It's very small and quite unorganized. We gather a few people from various segments of society and meet about once a week. We do a few basic things. First, we try to pray for the country. We have university students, kids, professionals, businessmen, poor Palestinians, and anyone else who wants to meet. These groups reflect Lebanon's society, so they're a mix of Muslim, Christian, and Druze. We all say we believe in a God who can save people, so we thought we'd start where we agree—prayer! But lately we've realized we need more than prayer. We need something to bind us together. Something to focus on. To study. So we decided to study the life of a great person who we would all agree on."

I paused, not wanting to do all the talking, and asked if he could suggest someone to study.

"Mother Teresa."

"Wow, Mother Teresa is one of my heroes," I said. "She's amazing. Anyone else you can think of that would work?"

He thought for a while, taking this very seriously, and replied, "What about Gandhi?"

"You've picked two of my three favorite historical leaders ever to live. I love Gandhi. Big fan. You know . . . I think these two people got a lot of their thinking from someone even further back, though. Sure you can't think of anyone else that might be good for our friends here to meet around?"

He must have thought for a full minute. All of a sudden he pounded the table—scared me half to death—and said, "I've got it. It's Jesus!" He nearly yelled it. Then he explained: "Muslims like Jesus. Druze like Jesus. Even

Christians like Jesus." (I'm not making that up—that's exactly what he said, "Even Christians . . .")

"Of course," I replied. "Really. Jesus, eh? Hmm. Could be. I think you're on to something here. Are you saying that you think everyone loves and respects Jesus, although possibly not the religion of his followers?"

"Exactly!" he burst out. "That's what I'm saying. We would all love to meet and discuss Jesus. Hey, we should do one of these groups in the parliament. You can lead it."

And so we did—we started a little gathering in the Lebanese parliament. It didn't change the world. It didn't change Lebanon. I don't even know if it changed us. But it was good. We didn't meet every week, but we met often, and when we were together it was wonderful. We studied through the gospel of Luke.

Once again, I saw that while Muslims are often afraid of Christianity and maybe even Christians, they're more than willing to look seriously into the life of Christ.

A CHRISTLIKE PERSPECTIVE

I want to close this chapter with a point that I hope will guide you and keep you. It can empower you, teach you, and, above all, give you confidence in the eyes of the world and in the eyes of God.

First of all, we have the greatest commandment: Love God and love people. Love has always been and will always be the strongest force in the universe. No one can stand against it. Not the worst Muslim or the best Christian. It is who God is and who he wants us to be. Love. (See 1 John 4:7–8.)

But there is something more. Read through the first chapter of Joshua to see what God commanded the children of Israel: "Be strong and courageous! *Do not be afraid*" (NLT emphasis added). Jesus himself, in the Gospels, said, "Do not fear those who kill the body…but rather fear Him who is able to destroy both soul and body in hell" (Matthew 10:28 NASB).

I hope these verses instill in you the priority of heaven about how you govern your heart. Yet it shouldn't stop there. Practicing the lifestyle of fearlessness toward the world with the proper fear of God will allow you to see several things very clearly.

For one thing, you will come to realize (if you haven't already) that you can be spiritual without being religious. The spirit carries weight with God; religion carries weight with people. "The mind set on the flesh is death, but the mind set on the Spirit is life and peace" (Romans 8:6 NASB).

You will also come to develop confidence in God's ability to save people. This is why I stopped making it my mission to "convert" anyone to the things that I thought were important. I learned that by following the Holy Spirit and being obedient to the teachings of Jesus, I could watch God save a person. I learned that it is the Spirit's responsibility to bring people to himself, and not mine.

I have discovered that when I fear God, there is no room in my heart to be afraid of men. When I fear God I don't

MUSLIMS, CHRISTIANS, AND JESUS

care about a loss of reputation or a fear of the future. I am secure. This allows me to be non-defensive, gentle, and above all, Christ-focused.

Finally, I pray that you too can find Jesus in the eyes and heart of your Muslim friend; that you can see him as a child searching for his father; and that you can take him by the hand and walk the journey of life and faith together—one step at a time.

A STORY OF FAITH

A Man as a Bridge

Abou Hamza (not his real name) is a friend of mine. He is a Sunni Muslim who lives in an extremely conservative Arab country. Most would say he lives in an Islamic fundamentalist context, maybe in its heartland.

I met Abou Hamza in Beirut, around 1998, at a gathering of mutual friends. He was fun, smart, articulate, and very wealthy. We talked now and then over the next year when he came to Beirut, but our friendship didn't grow much.

In 1999, though, I helped point his son to Jesus. That changed things. His son immediately and dramatically changed in all ways good. Abou Hamza was forever indebted.

It's actually a long story of patience and friendship (on both our parts). He saw me as a fairly typical Christian preacher, despite my best efforts to wear neither label. I saw him as a rough-and-tough rich

businessman, politically connected and entrenched in
everything Sunni. He was nearly twenty years my elder.
I was in over my head. He was not really someone I felt
qualified to mentor or disciple. But God is clever.

Soon we were spending time together all over the
world. In his country. In Lebanon. In the U.S. and En-
gland. In other Arab countries. In his words, he "started
loving the teachings of Jesus" and soon found himself
"loving Jesus."

My Christian friends were all excited for me. I'd done
it. I had led a prominent Arab Muslim to Jesus. My first
convert of notoriety.

In fact, Abou Hamza himself has a funny story
related to this. I was with him when he gave a lecture (in
English) at a renowned Arab university about business
ethics. I was so proud of him as he talked about following the way of Jesus Christ in all dealings. The audience
of thirty or so young professionals seemed surprised but
encouraged by the talk.

Two newspapers wrote stories about his lecture the
following day. The one with a Christian staff used the
"Christian" word in Arabic for Jesus (Yesua), saying
that Mr. Abou Hamza taught from the life of Yesua.
The other paper, with a Muslim staff, used the Qur'anic
word for Jesus (Isa).

You can almost guess what happened. He was
quickly inundated with phone calls from his friends.
His Christian friends, who had read *that* version of
the talk, called and said, "Ya Abou Hamza. Welcome
to the club. You've finally seen the light and become a

Christian." His Muslim friends, who read *their* newspaper, congratulated my friend that he had finally let those Christians know and understand a few things about who Jesus really is.

How funny is that. Everyone thinking they own Jesus.

Abou Hamza continued to grow in his love for Jesus—first in his teachings, and then it seemed to take on new life as Abou Hamza began to want to live and act and talk like Jesus. His words and actions changed. He softened. Business dealings were even more different. He was a changed man from the inside out.

When we were in the West together, he would talk about Jesus so passionately and personally with my friends that they couldn't help but ask, "So when did you become a Christian?"

He would smile and try to explain. "I'm a Muslim, but I follow Jesus. I believe in Jesus. I live for Jesus. He is everything to me."

They would push and ask questions like, "Yes, but when did you pray the prayer of salvation and ask Jesus into your heart?"

At first such inquiries would confuse him, as he had never heard that language before, but he soon caught on to cultural nuances and would reply with something like, "Jesus has captured me in stages. But I'm still a work in progress. Are *you* finished yet?" Then he'd flash a disarming smile and my friends would melt, knowing they had possibly asked the wrong question—or the right one in the wrong way.

The real issue for Abou Hamza was in trying to figure

out how to live out this new life in Christ within his context. It seems that one of two things happens when a Muslim in a conservative country comes to Christ. He either moves to the West, where he can live out his faith within Christian surroundings, or he stays and lives with his faith undercover, in fear that he will be ostracized or even killed.

But is there a third way? Can they stay in their own country, not have to live in hiding, and still talk openly about Jesus? It is possible! Abou Hamza has done it well.

The key that he and others have found is to live and speak in a way that allows their countrymen to embrace what they have experienced without their feeling like he has changed cultures or rejected his heritage. It's often not an issue of faith but of culture. When Muslims become "Christian," they're seen as traitors. This would be like a Navajo deciding to become a Hopi, says my friend from Arizona; it's impossible for a Navajo father to comprehend such a thing! Muslims who become "Christian" are not persecuted (usually) because of their deepened commitment to God, but because they've joined "the other side."

What Abou Hamza has done so well is to make every attempt to live out his life in a way that feels culturally Muslim to his friends while still being bold about his commitment to Jesus Christ. He lets everything go that would seem to be Christian in culture. Some of those things would be (according to him, at least): praying with head bowed and eyes closed, singing worship songs, quoting the chapter and verse when saying a Scripture, going to a church building on Sunday, etc.

When people hear Abou Hamza's story, they often ask if he still goes to mosque on Fridays and reads the Qur'an. Good questions. He does attend the mosque infrequently because it's the center for all things cultural. Weddings and funerals, as well as general community gatherings, happen at the mosque. To not go there would mean that he no longer values his friends and family. There's no reason to not go.

He feels that reading the Qur'an is tantamount to other Christians reading some other good book. It's not bad, but it doesn't bring the life that the Bible brings. Frankly, I think he reads the Qur'an less and less as he finds more and more fulfillment in the sixty-six books we call the Holy Scriptures.

Abou Hamza has become a bridge by his very life. He stands between two worlds. It's a precarious place to live. But it's the "new citizenship" of the people like Cornelius in the Bible. They join with Jews and people of every culture to become what the book of Acts calls the people of "the Way" (9:2; 19:23; 24:14; 24:22). He is from a culture and of a religion that has little tolerance for someone changing their way and joining another religion and culture. He is Muslim with his Muslim friends and can look and feel Christian with his Christian friends. But in the end he is a follower of Jesus. He translates Jesus into his culture and translates a new vision of Jesus into ours.

Thank you, Abou Hamza. All of us owe you a great

debt. As Paul wrote to the Corinthians two thousand years ago, "I have become all things to all men so that by all possible means I might save some. I do all this for the sake of the gospel" (1 Corinthians 9:22–23).

CHAPTER 8

Love Your Neighbor: Practical Ways to Reach Out to Muslims

The whole message of God can be summarized in one short sentence: Love God and love people. Eight times in the Bible we are told to "love your neighbor." It's one of the most repeated commands. And it's clear from the teachings of Jesus that our "neighbor" is basically anyone we meet who is in need (which would be everyone).

As we've discussed, Jesus seems to have a favorable bias toward the "wrong crowd." I hate to say it, but Muslims probably fit into this category! They're outsiders here in the

West: wrong religion, wrong language, wrong temperament. Sounds like Jesus' kind of people.

In this chapter I'll try to summarize this entire book, to bring it home. Literally. More and more people are finding they have Muslims living near them or working with them. That's wonderful in so many ways! Muslims will generally be your best neighbors. They're kind and thoughtful, they like to have fun, and they love good food—sharing it too.

Here I will share five practical thoughts on how to reach out in friendship in the name of Jesus to a Muslim neighbor or co-worker. I'll illustrate each with a story and leave you to work it out in your own situation.

THOUGHT ONE: HAVE FUN!

Have a good time. This advice is worth the price of this book, actually. It always amazes me how often those of us from Christian backgrounds (especially the more conservatives types) don't know how to party. In fact, that very word makes some nervous. Part of our excuse is that we're dealing with a life-and-death topic—our relationship with God. Fair enough.

Sometimes I've wondered if I've replaced being a vibrant witness of Jesus with cheap, lifeless imitations. A bumper sticker or fish on my car. A large King James Bible on the mantel. A picture of Jesus over the fireplace. And several pretty paintings with verses on them hung in strategic locations around the house so everyone will "know."

None of these things are bad. But they're not particularly deep or meaningful to a person walking into your house. What they likely say to the new neighbor is that you're religious.

What if your house were known on your street (and by your Muslim neighbors) as a party house? *If you want to have FUN, go to the Medearises'. They really know how to throw a bash. Great music. Fine food and beverages. Games in the basement. Big backyard with a volleyball net, a fire pit, and a killer barbecue.*

The one thing we do have to be careful of is not having alcohol and pork around if there are conservative Muslims. Other than that, the sky's the limit.

I remember New Year's Eve 2000. We were at our closest friend's house in downtown Beirut bringing in the New Year. About one hundred of our best Muslim friends were there. Loud music by a live band was rocking the chandelier. People danced. Almost every guy had a large Cuban cigar in his mouth and plenty to drink—some of which was normally forbidden. At midnight it was so loud I couldn't hear myself think, but when the noise died down a bit later, my first thought was, *Wow. Who would believe this? If someone had told me fifteen years ago that I was going to Beirut to be a witness of the Good News to Muslims, I would* not *have pictured* this!

And right in the middle of that atmosphere, Jesus was being lifted up. In the corners around the room, I saw people talking and praying. Later in the night we "prayed in" the

New Year. There was love. Community. Friendship. Stuff of the kingdom. All in the midst of an otherwise fairly wild party (not in inappropriate ways).

Learning point: If you don't know how to party, get help from someone who does. My friend Samir (the host) has often told me that I brought him an understanding of Jesus and that he brought me an understanding of how to have fun. I'd say that's true! But you also must know and understand needful boundaries and cultural norms so you don't offend more people than you win.

THOUGHT TWO: HAVE NO AGENDA

I know, we all have an agenda. Jesus had one. His was multifaceted. To serve. To teach twelve. To live in a way we could see the Father. To love. To die. And it seems the people he met never felt "used" by him. He never left a sinful woman or a blind beggar with a bad taste in their mouth. He looked people in the eye. Stopped during his busy day. Touched the leper and allowed the prostitute to wash his feet. When he healed or delivered people, he usually told them not to tell anyone. I know when I do something really cool, I tell everyone. Hmm.

But what if our "agenda" really is just to do good and serve people? In Jesus' name, of course. Not to convert them or fix them or save them. Just love them. Sort of like the title of this chapter, "Love Your Neighbor."

This doesn't mean we're not bold or that we don't share

this amazingly Good News we have. Quite the opposite. It's impossible to keep our mouths shut when our hearts are full. But we should not be in a hurry to "pray the prayer" with them. Or to "lead them to Jesus." We should simply be willing to be like Jesus, talk like Jesus, and love like Jesus. This means we shovel their sidewalks (which I have plenty of opportunities to do here in Denver); we pick up their kids from school when they need it; we smile a lot and have chats at the mailbox in the afternoons; and whenever and however we can, we bring up the Love of our Life. Not to "get 'em," but just because.

Possibly the best and worst story I have is this one. Ten of us were in Beirut having a team meeting at our house. We had prayed and worshiped and now were into our "strategy time." We were talking about how to reach Beirut for God. Then our doorbell rang. It was Hisham. *Oh no.* He was one of "them." A Muslim neighbor. One of those people we were strategizing about how to reach.

I kept the door half closed and awkwardly said, "Hi, what's up?"

Looking around the door and seeing several other friends, Hisham said, "Hey, are you having fun without me?" and walked right in. He greeted the people he knew and asked what we were doing.

"Well, nothing much," I lied. "Just, uh, praying and stuff. . . ."

So he sat down. Our group didn't know what to do. We talked to him, of course, but it was obvious we were all a bit annoyed. After all, we had busy schedules and only another half hour before the meeting ended and we could get on with life (reaching Beirut).

Hisham must have felt the tension because he left after twenty minutes. When he was gone, we all felt sick. We knew what had happened, but it was too late to catch ourselves.

Ironically and mercifully, God brought Hisham back the next week at exactly the same time. This time, I invited Hisham in, sat him down, and told him, "You know, many of us have left our countries and families to come to Beirut to see how God might want to bless this city and the nation of Lebanon. Any chance you could help us figure out how God might want to do this?" He was wild with excitement and ended up being one of my closest friends and partners!

If you want to evaluate your motives, ask yourself if you really just want the best for others, or if there's a hidden benefit in it for you as you "serve" people. Your Muslim friends will be particularly tuned in to any self-serving agenda if you have one. Just love them. It's enough.

THOUGHT THREE: BE A-RELIGIOUS

This advice to be "a-religious" (in other words, don't be religious), has bits and pieces of Thoughts One and Two wrapped up in it, but I want to highlight a few things I haven't yet mentioned.

After a talk I gave at Harvard one day, a Jewish grad student came to meet with me. She walked in loaded and ready for a fight. The first comment from her lips was, "I want you to know that I'm Jewish, and I don't believe that Jesus was the Messiah." She sat down with an air of self-confidence that made me feel like a small worm.

"Okay. By the way, my name's Carl. What's yours?"

"Melissa. But what do you *think*?"

"Think about what?"

"About Jesus *not* being the Messiah," she said with a bit of exasperation.

"Oh, that's fine. I'm actually not his defense attorney. You can think of him however you like."

She looked at the other three people in the room, who all seemed a little shocked by my non-response response. (I guess they were thinking I was on their "team," and their team didn't typically answer that way.) I could tell that Melissa was almost hoping for a good round or two with me in the ring of apologetics. She had certain answers ready for the answers she thought I'd give. So, why go there, I thought. That would be no fun at all (which would violate Thought One above).

She pushed. "Well, *do* you think he's the Messiah?"

"Actually, it doesn't matter all that much what I think about such lofty things. I suppose it matters what Jesus thought about who he was, but whatever I think won't change much of anything."

Not buying it, she asked, "Okay, so if you did think something about that, what would you be thinking? If you were going to prove to me that he was the Messiah, what's your best point?"

"I don't have a best point," I insisted.

"Well, then, why in the world am I here?"

"To be honest, I don't know. You came to me. Tell me why you came."

"I came to talk to you about why Jesus isn't the Messiah and to hear your points to refute that." She was getting desperate.

"Oh, sorry. Maybe you got the wrong guy. I'm not really into 'proving' things. Maybe we could talk about something else, though," I said honestly.

She said one last time: "Well, *if* you were going to give me your best shot about Jesus, what would it be?"

I could see there was a bit of real question in this one, so I answered, "He likes you."

She rolled her eyes. "Well, that's stupid. *That's* your best shot?"

"Yep. I told you I didn't have a best shot, but you wouldn't believe me."

She sat there shaking her head, mumbling something about "he likes me."

And then she started to cry. After a bit, she gathered herself and said defensively, "Well, I still don't believe he's the Messiah." I just smiled.

(Story update: This young woman has since been in a study of the Gospels with a group of friends at Harvard and is close to the kingdom.)

When I say "Don't be religious," I have several things in mind:

1. Don't be defensive. You have nothing to defend. God doesn't need help with his reputation, and the Bible can stand on its own. The defensive one in an argument is usually the one who is standing on shaky ground. Religious people are defensive.

2. Don't argue. Just don't. See what happens the next time someone says something you don't like or you don't agree with. Try just not arguing. No matter what. Religious people love arguments.

3. Don't carry yourself as if you know all truth. We know the One who is the Truth and, as we grow closer to him, we understand more. But how much of Jesus do you know? My guess is, I'm up to around 0.1 percent.

I've found that when I feel the need to defend Christianity, I dig myself a deep hole that is hard to escape. Christianity is a religion. I'm not religious. Islam is a religion. Judaism, Hinduism, and Buddhism are religions. Religions fight each other. They bicker and compete and try to win the other into their own. But we don't do that. We just lift up Jesus. We present him—the Good News. We follow him, love him, and serve him. But he wasn't very good at being religious either. So as we look to emulate Jesus, we try to stay far from the religious know-it-alls and close to the down-and-out sinner crowd.

THOUGHT FOUR: ADAPT TO THE RELIGIOUS FORMS OF YOUR MUSLIM FRIENDS

This is a tough one. The obvious follow-up question is, "How do we know the difference between what's Western Christian culture and the good stuff?" Great question. Answer: It's not easy to tell. Because no matter what we read and hear and believe, our experience supersedes it. As we're teaching things to our friends "directly from the Bible," what they're really picking up is what we do.

The person of Jesus—knowing him and understanding the Father—is the most positive force for change in the world. This is what Thomas Chalmers wrote in his historic sermon, "The Expulsive Power of a New Affection." Chalmers says that when Jesus is our new affection, prized above all other desires, he becomes a power in us that expels out from us all manner of sinful living. We who follow him have to have faith in him to change everyone in the world. But we may have unconsciously expected Muslims to adapt to our religious practices as well as to delight in Jesus.

A simple example of this would be how we pray. Muslims would do informal prayer probably standing, with their eyes open and their hands in front of them, palms up. Of course we know that "real" prayer happens with heads bowed and eyes closed. But, for as much as I've tried to not impose my style, I now see most of my Muslim friends who have come to Christ praying with their heads bowed and eyes closed.

This is not bad, it's just not the point. We teach who we are. You can see it in different kinds of churches too. Some churches are sure they have to speak loudly with great animation for God to hear. Others are obviously convinced that God can read minds, because you will never hear a peep from them. Some raise hands. Others bend knees. Some preachers speak without notes for an hour while others memorize a ten-minute homily. Some dance. Some would never think of moving. Hard benches. Soft chairs. Choirs. Rock bands. Steeples and stained glass. And some even think they can meet God in homes. And what's funny is they all back up their cultures with Scripture.

It gets more complicated when you get into questions like "What makes a church?" Elders? Deacons? Senior pastor and staff? Mega-church vs. two or three gathered in a coffee shop? Members voting. Pastors ruling. Breaking bread weekly. Monthly. Baptizing all and often. Dipping, dunking, or sprinkling. All proved by Holy Writ.

And what do you need to believe in order to be "in"? This one's really tough. I was raised to believe that you needed to say "The Sinner's Prayer." Some would say that the prayer is needed, plus a public confession in baptism. Others would argue that those aren't enough—we likewise need correct doctrine. Which doctrine? Well, theirs of course. Basic things like justification by faith alone. Salvation by grace.

Substitutionary atonement. Repentance. And then some say even all that's not quite enough until you're baptized in the Holy Spirit.

So, back to the question at hand. How do we know which things are just part of our cultural upbringing and which things are really necessary to be sharing with our friends? Here's my list of must-share things:

1. Jesus

Not much of a list, is it?

Some would say, "Carl, you have to give us more than that."

Really? More than Jesus? I would just ask that you share things about Jesus that are true. That are real. That make sense. Things he's done in your life. Things from the sixty-six books we call the Bible. Those things. Share them in some sort of logical order. Probably don't start at the end of the story. Allow the story to unfold naturally. For my wife and me, that means:

1. We talk about Jesus in every nonreligious way possible. I often say things like, "You know . . . Jesus. That guy who lived in the Middle East two thousand years ago. You know . . . that guy." Or I'll say something like, "I grew up in a conservative Christian home but realized I didn't like Christianity much as a religion. But I'm afraid I may have thrown the baby (Jesus) out with the dirty bath water of Christianity. So I'm trying to

figure out how to get him back and let the rest go." Or I tell them what I do: I explain that I try to bring reconciliation between Muslims, Christians, and Jews by teaching the principles of Jesus. All fairly non-typical thoughts about our faith and how we express it.

2. We get involved in their lives. This takes (precious) time. We get to know their kids. We invite them around whenever we can. We cancel everything when they call.

3. We would never invite them to a Bible study. Christians do Bible studies. No one else in the world sits around and studies a book. We invite them to a discussion group (which is what we've just done with our neighbors). We let others lead. We don't control it when the group wanders. We're simply studying this interesting and controversial figure of history—Jesus. I try hard not to sound like a salesman for him.

4. We try to bring in the neighbors on the decision to meet. We've been talking to our neighbors nonchalantly about this for months. Things like, "Hey, we should get the cul-de-sac together and talk about this stuff sometime." When we decided to do it, we went to the other family on the street that we thought would have the most clout and asked them if they'd meet with us. When they said yes, we went to the other families individually over a few weeks and enlisted

their support of the idea. We'd say something like, "Hey, Rob, Krista, and we were thinking of having a little discussion group to talk about the life of Jesus. Maybe meet at our house, or wherever, and look at different things about him that we might find relevant to our lives. I don't know . . . just a thought . . . what do you think?"

5. We remember that these people are worth more than our plans. Therefore, if it doesn't work at first, just drop it and try again later. Or do something else with the one couple who might come. Or whatever . . . just don't force your plan.

The Basra Sheikh

I jumped out of our rented white Suburban in downtown Basra, Iraq, and yelled, "Who's in charge here?"

We do this sort of thing.

A crowd formed instantly, and it was quickly apparent that someone named Sheikh Ali was the Big Man in town. By our third minute in Basra I found myself in the backseat of a stranger's black Mercedes going to meet a man I'd never heard of—the leading Shi'ite cleric of southern Iraq.

Sheikh Ali's domain was the largest mosque in the city; it easily rivaled the largest church campuses in the

States. Among other things, there was a school, a college, a sheikh training center, and housing for the poor.

Sheikh Ali was presiding over a large gathering of other Islamic leaders when we arrived, but in the good fashion of Arab hospitality he immediately stood up when he saw the four of us at the door and left his meeting to greet us.

"What are you doing here?" he asked. A fair question to ask an American in Iraq in May of 2003.

"Well, I'm not very good at it, but I'm trying to follow Jesus, and we've come here looking for him. Have you seen him?" (That got his attention.) "We were in Lebanon a few weeks ago praying, and the thought came to us that Jesus might be in Iraq. Two thousand years ago he was always where the religious leaders of his day thought he wouldn't be. Have you seen him?" I repeated.

The sheikh squinted over the top of his reading glasses, ruffled his beard, leaned toward his friends with a slight smile, and said, "Interesting question. No, we've not seen Jesus, but maybe the question should be, *If he were here, what would he be doing?*"

I was stunned. Maybe he had a WWJD bracelet. How'd he know *that* question? And then Sheikh Ali and his under-sheikhs were off and running with the question.

We batted the idea around for about thirty minutes, until they announced with an air of finality, "He'd be helping the children and taking care of the poor. Therefore, if Jesus would be doing that, maybe we should give more attention to the poor and to children—specifically, poor children." Sheikh Ali looked at me and smiled. "That was a good question you asked."

I basically said the next thing that came to my mind. "I have some more really good news for you. Do you know that if you were my enemy, that'd be a good thing for you?" I think I was two for two on weird questions!

"How's that?"

"Well, Jesus clearly says to do three things with your enemies: love them, bless them, and pray for them. He said that anyone can love their friend or brother, but loving an enemy seems to be a higher and more noble thing. So . . . you're not my enemy, but if you were, that'd be good since I'd basically be obliged by the One I follow to love, bless, and pray for you."

Sheikh Ali really liked that one. He stood up, pulled his large hand from beneath his long black robe, and said, "Well, then, your enemy I'll be," and he burst into a huge grin and hugged me.

Following no set order of progression, I decided to tell them the story of the Good Samaritan, where Jesus once again makes "good" guys look bad and "bad" guys look good. You know it: A man finishes his prayers in Jerusalem and is walking home when he's beaten up, robbed, and left for dead. Two "good" guys—a priest and a Levite—are too busy doing good-guy things to stop and help. But a "bad" guy—a hated foreigner—stops and spends a lot of time and money helping a stranger.

With the sheikh, I personalized the story and said

that if it were set in Basra today, I would be one of the good guys and he'd be the bad guy. In fact, I went so far as to jokingly tell him that if my friends knew I was meeting with him, they'd be praying really hard since he's the bad guy and I'd need lots of help as the good guy to overcome his badness. He not only got the joke but promised to relay it to others!

In the spirit of the story, he got up and extended his hand and said, "This is my city, and I give it to you and your friends. Whatever you want to do here I'll help. Come and stay with me. You can store your humanitarian supplies here. I'll tell everyone that you're okay and not to mess with you."

I jumped on this. "See," I said, "you're like the Good Samaritan to me. You're turning the table upside down and treating me like a brother. I came to help you, but you're helping me."

(Story update: This man has stayed faithful to his promise and has truly become a man of peace for the city of Basra.)

THOUGHT FIVE: BE YOURSELF

This one is tougher than it looks. It's amazing how much time we spend being someone else. I've done it much of my life. Even in our attempt to be like Jesus, we're asked to be "like" him in our own skin. We're all uniquely created to act and think in different ways. It's part of God's beautiful mosaic of the world.

One of the things I love most about Jesus is that he wasn't phony. It almost sounds funny to say it—but he was himself. And he's not that easy to define. We should also be multidimensional. Deep. Full of integrity and with many sides.

Have you ever noticed that people have incredible phony-o-meters? They can smell a charlatan one thousand miles away. That's why we don't like phony salespeople. It's not that they're selling us something. The whole world is doing that. And maybe we even need what they're selling. It's that they don't believe in their product. They talk fast. Have way too many facts lined up. And they're not even sure we really need their product.

We're automatically suspicious of salespeople because we know it's their *job*. They're paid to convince us. But what if they were doing it for no money? We'd be more apt to buy. *Wow, they must really believe in this if they're doing it on their own time,* we'd think.

I was with a friend from Sudan the other day. He was visiting me here in Denver, and we got to talking about the usual stuff. Jesus and . . . well, I can't remember the other stuff. Our conversation in my pickup truck went something like this:

"Carl, I love introducing you to my other Muslim friends because they always leave feeling encouraged. You're just so natural with them."

"Well," I said, trying to look deep and thoughtful, "I don't know what else to do but be myself. If I can encourage them and talk about the things that matter most in life, then that's awesome."

"Yeah, but I've been around a lot of people who are trying to convert me to their way of thinking, and it just turns me and my friends off. Somehow you don't do that, but we still always end up talking about Jesus and reading the Bible. You're either good or very sneaky."

"I've tried being sneaky and it just didn't work for me. I've tried being someone else and that didn't work either. So I thought I'd just be myself and see how that goes."

Last week I had an all-too-common conversation with a missionary. He wanted my take on how he should approach ministry in his Muslim context. At first, he had gone in with guns blazing, so to speak. He was a "Christian missionary there to convert Muslims."

He had integrity. He was just being honest. Up-front. Forthright. After a couple of years, though, he realized his message actually didn't have integrity because no one understood it. (It doesn't matter what we think we're saying—it's what others hear.)

So he changed tactics. He'd be a tentmaker. After all, the apostle Paul made tents. My friend didn't know how to make tents, but he had taken a business class in college, so he thought he'd start a little coffee shop. (This story is real, by the way, but I've had similar exchanges a hundred times and more.)

He worked really hard. So hard that he was exhausted. He now had a clear identity. He wasn't a Christian missionary anymore; he was now a business owner. A real, legitimate businessman. Of course, he was working seventy hours a week and had no time for his family, let alone his neighbors. And now he'd given up all that "Christian evangelism stuff" and was trying to be much more "natural" in his new role as a businessman. But he was noticing he hadn't really shared any part of his faith for a while—partly because he was so busy and partly because he didn't know how to talk about Jesus without being in a religious role.

His story is the story of so many. My response to him was what I've said to so many friends: How about if you just be who you are? Here's what I mean:

1. *Share Jesus only when you want to.* Hold on. Don't freak out. Let me explain. So many of my friends are sharing Jesus because they feel obligated to. I equate that with loving Chris because she's my wife. What if I love her because I do? Wouldn't that be better? What if I told her I love her because I do love her, and it's real, rather than telling her I love her because that's what I learned at the marriage seminar. Of course the tricky part of this is that I have to actually love her. And I have to want to share Jesus because I love him

and because he's done so much in my life and in the lives of my friends.

2. *Do what you're good at doing.* I'm a horrible manager of people. When I try, I hurt them and me. I'm good at thinking. Envisioning things. Getting things going. But I'm awful at keeping them going. I've tried on the hats of "businessman," "humanitarian worker," "missionary," and "the guy who hangs out and drinks coffee." I've taken the personality tests. The gift tests. I know what letters I am. ENTP. Hi D. Type A. Messed up, I'd say. Trying to hang out, but really just driven. Point is—if you are a businessperson, do business. If you're not—don't. If you live to serve the poor, then be a humanitarian worker with World Vision. If you don't—don't.

3. *Say what you believe.* Because I actually believe this stuff I've written, I tell people right up front something like, "I don't have a religious bone in my body, but I sure think Jesus is awesome. I'm pretty sure you'd like him too if you got to know him." I even say, "I used to be a Christian missionary, and then I met Jesus. Now I just try to follow him. I find that's enough." They have no idea what that means, which is fun, because it leads to great conversations.

BASIC DOS AND DON'TS

I've shared much of this before, but it might help to see it as a list. So here goes, some basic dos and don'ts:

1. Never attack the person of Muhammad or the Qur'an. These are the most sensitive topics to a Muslim, and they should be avoided if possible until a real relationship is established.

2. Feel free to visit your local mosque. They'll love it. Guaranteed. For more insight how, see page 182.

3. Try not to use the terms *Son of God*, *Christian*, or *church*. Try to explain each of these by the realities they represent rather than the term or phrase itself. (Again, it's not that I don't believe in the realities that these words represent, but the words themselves are unhelpful.)

4. It is important to treat the Bible with total respect. Never place it on the ground. Always open and close it carefully. Muslims are often shocked at how we treat God's Holy Word. (In the same way, show respect for the Qur'an.)

5. Respect Jesus by using his name with a title. For instance, refer to him as Jesus the Christ (Messiah). This is a term Muslims recognize and accept.

6. In the month of Ramadan, try not to eat on the streets or in front of Muslims.

7. Never walk in front of a praying Muslim.

8. Stand, kneel, or hold out your hands with your palms upward when praying.

9. Women should dress modestly around Muslims. (This is actually a biblical concept too, but Muslims take it more seriously than we do.)

10. Women should not offer to shake the hand of a Muslim man. If he offers his hand, then it's okay.

11. Never assume you know what a Muslim believes. Always ask him or her.

12. Feel free to read the Qur'an. It's not a bad book, and it mostly agrees with the Bible.

13. Avoid politics if at all possible. This is always going to be a hot button with a Muslim; you can never "win" this argument.

14. Be aware that pork, alcohol, and dogs are "dirty" in Islam and are to be avoided by Muslims at all times.

15. Avoid showing the bottom of your feet.

16. Never use your left hand to shake or eat with.

17. Express sadness at the state of Western morals and spirituality. Make a clear distinction between the "Christian West" and what a true follower of Jesus looks like.

18. Always offer to pray for your Muslim friend. Muslims have a great deal of respect for prayer and for people of prayer. Pray for blessing on their family, work, and home. Invite God's Spirit to come and touch them. Pray right then, out loud.

19. Share from personal experience. Tell stories. Be real.

20. Talk about your family and ask about theirs. They are family people.

21. Above all—listen. Be a good listener. You will win the heart of anyone when you listen!

A STORY OF FAITH

An Unfair Advantage

About a year ago I was invited to participate in a citywide discussion hosted by a church on the topic of interfaith dialogue. Several hundred people crowded the hall as the introductions were made. The introductions basically went like this: "The honorable Muslim sheikh, the imam Yusef el Ahmadi, leader of the Colorado Springs Islamic Society." Then, "The doctor, sheikh, leading thinker, Imam Ali bin Muhammad, president of the American Muslim Society of Imams [and other really important things]." Then came two rabbis: "The rabbi Yossi Guren of the [insert name of synagogue that sounds very important, which I can't remember]" and "the first lady rabbi in Colorado, founder and president of the [most amazing something that's ever been started, which I can't remember]." Finally, they introduced a bishop who was and is immortalized as the Catholic leader of the Colorado Springs area.

Then the host came to me and said—this is no lie— "And finally we have . . . uh . . ."

"Carl. The name's Carl." He was obviously embarrassed that he didn't know my title or my great accomplishments—of which I have neither. So he just said, "Mr. Carl," and everyone laughed.

Each of us were to respond to two questions that evening. The first was, "How does your religion get you to heaven?"

The two Muslim guys did a fine job articulating the various Islamic views on what it takes to get into heaven, which comes down to the "will of God." The two Jewish rabbis explained their uncertainty of life after death, and therefore their focus on this life now. The Catholic bishop did well with helping us understand the various interpretations within Christianity of the afterlife and how to get to heaven.

Then it was my turn. I was praying for something significant to say. This is what came out: "Actually, my religion doesn't get you to heaven." The other panelists shifted uncomfortably in their chairs, and the host asked if I'd like to explain more.

"Sure," I said. "I've just never seen a religion save anyone. All religions are great at laying out some basic rules—dos and don'ts—that are good for our lives, but they don't really provide hope or any kind of eternal security. It seems religions end up causing more trouble than solving anything."

"So then," said the host, "how do you get to heaven?"

This all seemed so basic, but I thought I might as well go ahead and say the obvious. "Well, it's Jesus. He didn't start a new religion; he came to provide us a model for life and a way to God. Believing in and following him is the way. *He* takes us to heaven, not a religion."

Next came question number two: "How does your religion deal with terrorism?"

The two Muslims felt a little defensive with this question but nicely denounced all forms of terrorism and explained how the Qur'an does not provide a place for it. The rabbis spent most of their time trying to convince the two Muslims that they had clearly misread their own book on the subject. And the bishop talked about mercy mixed with justice.

Me? I said, "I don't really know. I'm not sure how the religion I grew up in would or should deal with terrorism. But I do have some thoughts on how Jesus might deal with terrorists." My nerves seemed to be stealing my breath. "Jesus didn't deal much with the various 'isms' of his day. He had an uncanny way of dealing with the people themselves rather than the ideologies they represented. (With the arguable exception of the religious leaders.) So I'm not sure what Jesus would have done with terrorism, but I'm pretty sure we can see how he'd treat a terrorist, because he had two with him in his inner circle of friends: a zealot and a tax collector. A political insurgent and an economic terrorizer of the common folk. What he did with these two was bring them in as confidants. As students. Disciples. And he made them apostles of the early faith.

"It actually seems to me that the worse someone was, the more Jesus liked them. He didn't just have 'mercy' on them in the way we think of it—a sappy, lovey-dovey sort of thing. It was mercy with a bite. A mercy that led people out of where they were and into a new place. This is what Jesus did with the worst of them. He was only hard on one type of folks—people like us." I looked down the line and smiled. "People like me. Hypocrites and such."

Right about now I'm sure they were all wondering why they'd invited me. Twenty minutes of questions and answers followed, and then we wrapped it up.

Afterward, I had a small crowd around me asking questions. One lady was more than a little upset with me. "You didn't even mention the Trinity," she said.

"True," I replied, "but it didn't come up in the course of the conversation. . . ."

"But surely you do believe in the Trinity, don't you? And there are some other things you didn't mention that you should have, like the Atonement."

I knew I needed to tread lightly. Everyone lives in a

context, and it's good to be sensitive to the American Christian context as much as anyone else's context. So I simply said, "You're probably right; I believe everything in this book," and I held up my Bible, showing her that it appeared to be well-read.

Then a young man jumped into the conversation. "I'm a Muslim. I came with the imam tonight." He turned to the lady who had been speaking with me, and said, "If this man [pointing to me] had talked about theology or doctrine or even Christianity, I wouldn't have been interested. But he talked about Jesus in a way I've never heard before and had never thought of. I thought it was amazing."

To her credit, she said, "Wow, maybe you're right. I wonder if I've confused my religion with my Savior."

At that moment, the local imam came up. "Carl, Carl, Carl. You had an unfair advantage." He was smiling but also wagging his finger in my face. I wasn't sure where this was going.

"What's that, sir?" I asked a bit timidly.

"While we were all busy defending our religions and our positions, you simply talked about Jesus. You cheated!" Then he let out a huge laugh, slapped me on the back, and said, "Good job," before walking away.

I actually wonder if that sums it up. We have an unfair advantage. We know the Creator. We're friends with the King. We know where truth is found. We know what brings life and what gives life and where eternal life resides. While others are explaining and defending various "isms" and "ologies," we're simply pointing people to our Friend. The one who uncovers and disarms. Who leads people right to himself. The beginning and the end of the story.

GETTING TO KNOW THE MUSLIMS AROUND YOU

I often have people ask me how I got such a love for Muslims. My typical answer is, "I don't love Muslims." I love Samir and Ahmad and Ali and their families.

It's a funny idea that we can love a group of people or an ideology or a principle. Jesus seemed to love individual people.

Perhaps you already know some Muslims. You have them as your neighbors, co-workers, or fellow students. And maybe you've been a little shy in talking to them, but you know they're around. I'd guess this will be the case for more and more of us as Muslims grow in numbers through conversion, immigration, and birth.

If you already know a Muslim to some degree—get ready to highlight this—go and talk to him or her some more. Start with something easy like, "Hi, how are you?" And then move on to things like, "Where do you or your family originally come from?" Don't ask simply, "Where are you from?" Often immigrants are offended by that question since now they're "from" here. So adding the words *your family* and *originally* helps it feel a bit more friendly. If you want to be their friend, of course you'd want to know where they're from, so just ask.

I think I've found another amazing secret to winning people's trust and their hearts. Food. Not just any kind of food, but good food. And lots of it. If I can be direct, this is a real challenge for Americans. We aren't great at lavishing hospitality on people. We have been taught to only invite really close friends into our house. And if we do cook them dinner, often we make just enough to feed them—no leftovers is a good thing!

I have never been in a home for a meal in the Middle East where there wasn't at least twice as much food as needed. That's a good rule of thumb anyway: Cook twice as much as you think you'll need for the meal and then save the leftovers for lunch the next day.

Another thing: When Muslims come into your home, give them choices of fruit juice, soda, coffee, or tea. In many Eastern cultures it's polite to say no several times to an offer. So if you ask them if they want something to drink, they will almost surely say no. Don't bother asking. Just bring out several cold drinks and offer them around. If you say, "Do you want coffee or tea?" they will say no. But if you say that you have coffee and tea and you're just asking who wants the coffee or tea you already have, then it works.

It's really not hard. Just insist that they eat and drink as much as they can hold. Good food. Good beverages. And lots of it.

When inviting your new friends to your home: Just

be yourself. We had some Saudi students over a couple of weekends ago, and we served them all apple pie and ice cream for dessert. Not exactly a Middle Eastern dish, but they loved it.

Cook what you know how to cook. Remember, if they're from India and you decide to cook your best curry dish, it's not likely to taste like their mom's. So cook whatever your best dish is. But remember, no pork.

Feel free to say something like this when you sit down for the meal: "Our family has a tradition to honor God by saying thank-you for this food and for you. Do you mind if we do that?" They won't mind and will actually love it. They will keep their heads up and their eyes open, so don't let that distract you. In fact, I now typically pray with my head up and eyes open. Make the prayer natural, conversational, and real. I always find this is a highlight of the meal. Don't be afraid to pray!

Finally, as in all conversation with Muslims, let them know you're a person of faith. You may not be very "religious," but you do believe. They will respect this, as they are also people of faith. Let conversations develop naturally. Don't force things. Be real. Focus on your shortcomings and on their strengths. These are just basic people skills.

When you're comfortable, you can ask your new Muslim friend if he or she would like to meet once in a while to read the Scriptures together or talk about matters of life and faith. If they have time, they will want to. (Just like almost anyone else in the world.)

Don't be intimidated by not knowing the Qur'an. Your Muslim friends will feel about the Bible the way you feel about the Qur'an, so you'll both need to get over your insecurities. Make sense? Admit you're a dunce in need of tons of grace, and go for it. Try to keep the time focused (at least initially) on areas of agreement. If you've read this far, then you know that I think the number one thing we both agree on is Jesus. So focus on him. Maybe do a Jesus reading. Read all the passages about him in the Qur'an, and read the gospel of Luke. No agenda. Just read. The Holy Spirit has the agenda stuff covered, so you can relax and enjoy yourself.

If you don't know any Muslims but want to meet and talk with some, it's really quite easy to do. If you're a university student or live near a university, find out if there's a Muslim association of some kind and contact them. Many Muslims who study in America are lonely and have never been invited into an American home. Another way to learn about Islam and perhaps make new friends is to shop at a Middle Eastern or Asian food market. Muslims prepare their meat in a way that's similar to kosher standards. Halal food is tasty and good for you.

One final idea is to call your local mosque or Islamic center (look them up in the phone book under "Mosque" or "Islamic Center") and tell them you'd like to learn more about Islam and perhaps meet with some folks; ask when would be a good time to come by for a visit. I've done this quite a lot, and I've had 100-percent-positive response.

When visiting a mosque, there are really only two things to note: women are welcome, shoes are not. Take your shoes off when you go inside—there will be a place by the door to put them. If there isn't, ask the first person you see what to do with your shoes.

If you're a woman wanting to visit, you may not be able to go into certain areas, but either they'll instruct you or there will be a sign that says "Men Only." Other than that, women are welcome to go into the main building; ladies, you may have to sit on the side or in the back of the prayer area. (In some cases, women won't be able to go into the main prayer room, but again, just ask or look for a sign.)

FINAL THOUGHTS

Muslims are our friends. They're nice, likeable, easy-going, balanced people who respect God and others and enjoy life. They love their kids. They're concerned about the moral decay they see around them. They are pro-life, pro-family, and pro-faith. They work with us, go to school with our kids, shop at Wal-Mart, and eat at McDonald's. Muslims are allies in many of the local political issues you and I are passionate about. They dream for the same kind of life we dream of. They are friends!

In writing this book I've realized that I have two dreams for the reader. The first is that you would see Jesus a little more clearly. That he would become more tangible. More accessible in some way. That following him would be a little less theoretical and mystical and just a bit more practical or real.

Second, I hope that you would *see* Muslims. Jesus always saw people. He saw the lepers when no one else did. He saw the blind, the beggars, the women, the man who climbed the tree to see him. Jesus saw the seeker before the seeker saw him. Jesus looked for and saw people. And when he would see them—really see them—Jesus would always interact at their point of need.

So what is it that our Muslim neighbors need us to see in them? Maybe that they too were created in the image of God? Or that they are lonely in a foreign country? Misunderstood?

Will we cross the street as the Levite and the priest did or will we take the role of the Samaritan and see a person in need of grace? I think it's a real question—the answer is in our feet. Which way will they turn?

May we become more like our Master as we follow in his steps.

ABOUT THE AUTHOR

Carl Medearis has twenty-five years of firsthand experience working and living with Muslims. He is the founder and president of International Initiatives, which promotes cultural, educational, and commercial exchanges between East and West.

During his twelve years in Beirut, Lebanon, Carl formed relationships in Lebanon, Jordan, Iraq, and Saudi Arabia among businesspeople, parliamentary bodies, and university students. Through his unique approach, he teaches these leaders to live their lives by the principles of Jesus in order to change their nations. He built a community center in downtown Beirut for university students and for several years played a key role in the Lebanese nongovernmental organization Imma, which runs community centers around Lebanon in Palestinian refugee camps, working with and mentoring youth from grade-school age to university students.

In the United States, Carl leads the International Student Leadership Forum on Faith and Values, which convenes in Washington, D.C., and Denver, Colorado, and he has also developed a Web site (*www.faithdialog.com*) to create conversation between the East and the West.

As an advisor on Arab affairs, Carl travels with members of the U.S. Senate and House of Representatives, as well as senior leaders in international business on trips to the Middle East, helping them understand Arab culture and language and facilitating face-to-face meetings that break down prejudice and stereotypes.

Carl is one of the hosts to the Arab delegation at the annual National Prayer Breakfast in Washington, D.C., at the invitation of a bilateral committee of members of the U.S. Congress, who seek to discuss issues of peace and reconciliation based on shared beliefs in God and the teachings of Jesus of Nazareth.

Carl Medearis holds a Bachelor of Arts in history and a graduate degree in secondary education. He is a consultant for several institutions and universities and is a sought-after public speaker in the area of reconciliation between East and West.

Carl currently lives in Denver, Colorado, with his wife, Chris, and their three children. For more information, visit *www.carlmedearis.com.*

Statistics, Related Reading List, and Glossary of Terms

Christianity and Islam are the two most populous religions in the world, with Christianity having just over 2 billion adherents and Islam approximately 1.4 billion.

Arab countries comprise the largest demographic of Muslims at more than 280 million. Sub-Saharan Africa contains more than 250 million; Pakistan and Bangladesh have 230 million; and Indonesia has the highest Muslim population for an individual nation at 195 million. India has about 130 million Muslims and Iran has a Shi'a Muslim population of 65 million. Southeast Asia has about 100 million, central Asia and Azerbaijan have almost 50 million, and Russia has almost 30 million. Afghanistan has 23 million, whereas the United States and the European Union have fewer than 10 million each, and Latin America has 2 million or fewer.

RELATED READING LIST

These books are about sharing our faith with Muslims and/or focusing on Jesus. I don't necessarily agree with everything each author says, but what's the point of reading a new book if you already know and agree with the material. With that said, here are some interesting and provocative titles:

The Crescent Through the Eyes of the Cross by Nabeel Jabbour

The Christ of the Indian Road by E. Stanley Jones

Building Bridges: Christianity and Islam by Fouad Accad

Pilgrims of Christ on the Muslim Road: Exploring a New Path Between Two Faiths by Paul-Gordon Chandler

Who Speaks for Islam? What a Billion Muslims Really Think (a Gallup Poll book) by John Esposito and Dalia Mogahed

A Deadly Misunderstanding: A Congressman's Quest to Bridge the Muslim-Christian Divide by Mark Siljander

GLOSSARY OF TERMS

adhan	the call to prayer
ahl-al-kitab	the people of the book; Jews and Christians
Allah	God (lit: "the God")
arkan-ud-din	the pillars of religion
ayatollah	a religious leader in Shi'a Islam
caliph	a leader of the worldwide Muslim community
dhimmi	non-Muslim in a Muslim community, a second-class citizen
fatwa	a published decree or ruling regarding theology or legislation
hadji	a person who has made the pilgrimage
hajj	the annual pilgrimage to Mecca
hijab	the seclusion or concealment of women; also used to refer to the head-covering
iblis	the devil
imam	the leader of a mosque
iman	articles of faith
Injil	the Gospels and/or the whole New Testament
jihad	literally means "struggle" and can be used to mean "war." Fundamentalists generally believe this to be an additional pillar of faith.

jinn	spirits
jumma	Friday, the holy day of the week
Kaaba	the shrine of Mecca
mahdi	"rightly guided one," an expression used mainly by Shi'ites
mihrab	a notch in the wall of a mosque, indicating the direction of Mecca for prayers
mujahed	an Islamic warrior; mujahedin is plural
mullah	a religious teacher
nabi	prophet
qara	recitation, the origin of the word Qur'an
qibla	the direction of prayer
Qur'an	the principal holy book of Islam
Ramadan	the ninth month of the Islamic calendar, the month of the fast
salam	peace—used in greeting
salat	the daily ritual prayers
sawm	the act of fasting
Shahada	the testimony
Sharia	Islamic law
Shaytan	Satan
sheikh	leader, chief

Shi'a (or Shi'ite)	a sect of Islam that believes that Ali was the rightful successor to Muhammad
shirk	the unforgivable sin—to credit anyone to God's status
sufi	a Muslim mystic
Sunni	"one of the pathway," orthodox Islam. A majority sect that believes in elected imamate
surah	Qur'anic chapters
taqdir	predestination
tasbih	the Muslim rosary
Wahhabi	followers or sectarians who push puritanical reform
Zabur	the Psalms of David